Third Edition

JAZZ ENGLISH
Real Conversations
Real Improvement

2

NO RULES
JUST SPEAKING
LONG & LOUD

GUNTHER BREAUX

Compass Publishing

JAZZ ENGLISH 2 Third Edition

Gunther Breaux

© 2015 Compass Publishing

All rights reserved. No part of this book may be reproduced, stored in a retrieval system, or transmitted in any form by any means, electronic, mechanical, photocopying, recording, or otherwise without prior permission from the publisher.

Acquisition Editor: Peggy Anderson
Editor: Daniel Deacon
Design and layout: Gunther Breaux

ISBN: 978-89-6697-860-1

15 14 13 12 11 10 9
24

Photo Credits: pp. 18, 21, 46: Courtesy of Gunther Breaux
All other images © Shutterstock, Inc.

Websites: compasspub.com, jazzenglish.com

Every effort has been made to trace all sources of illustrations/photos/information in this book, but if any have been inadvertently overlooked, the publisher will be pleased to make the necessary arrangements at the first opportunity.

Printed in Korea

My Education

Any education in any major will teach you only two things:

1. How to tell a good idea from a bad idea.

2. How to express yourself.

Jazz English will give you the ability to express yourself.

By the end of this semester you will have a University Degree in Me.

Acknowledgments

Chris Kobylinski has greatly enhanced this book. His knowledge of American and Korean culture as well as his teaching experience and expertise make this book more interesting, authentic, and relevant. Daniel Deacon's contribution as editor includes much more than editing. His visual and artistic sense and teaching experience have helped every facet of this book. Also, Dan's British background broadens the relevance of this book.

Gratitude goes to my colleagues Jim Life, Mike Madill, Shaun Manning, and Todd Hull, who freely shared their expertise. I also appreciate the help given by the superb teachers and professors who use *Jazz English*: Jared Betts, Bryan Betz, Richard Cassidy, Katelyn Jones, Amelie Kelly, Robbie Sawlor, Ehren Schaiberger, Laurie Schulte, Nikki Slack, Marika Svaboda, and Jasmine Taiwo.

Finally, Kang, Gui-lim's expertise in teaching methodology and layout design, cultural insights, and translating skills have immeasurably helped this book.

Gunther Breaux has taught English conversation in Korea for eighteen years. He's an associate professor at Hankuk University of Foreign Studies in Seoul and the author of several ELT books. He has a BA in Advertising Design, an MA in American History, and an MA in TESOL. For eleven years he taught at Dongduk Women's University, and for five years he taught Business English part-time at Korea Development Institute (KDI). He has also taught Computer Graphics at the Korea National University of the Arts.

CONTENTS

PREVIEW & INSTRUCTIONS — 5

CHANGE THE MINDSET
First Week
    Real-World English — 10
    Speed Dating — 12

Second Week
    Classroom MT — 14
    Personality Test — 16

MAIN UNITS
  1 All About Me — 18
  2 Weekends & Neighborhoods — 26
  3 Technology — 34
  4 Dating & Nightlife — 42
  5 Sofa Time — 50
  6 Health & Fitness — 58
  7 Holidays, Festivals, & Feelings — 66
  8 Working & Getting There — 74

SUPPORT UNITS
  9 Pronunciation Practice & Konglish — 82
  10 Directions — 84
  11 Describing — 88
  12 Core Vocabulary — 96
  13 Core Skills — 100
  14 Explanations & Examples — 103
  15 Board Games — 130
  16 Maps: World, USA, Korea, Seoul — 139

There are over 300 questions in this book. Each question is designed to start a conversation. You know the answers because every question is about you. Just write your answer and use it to speak.

PREVIEW

DO THE BOOK AT HOME, SPEAK IN CLASS.

| Translated vocabulary | Pair activity: 16 conversation-starting questions | Model Conversation |

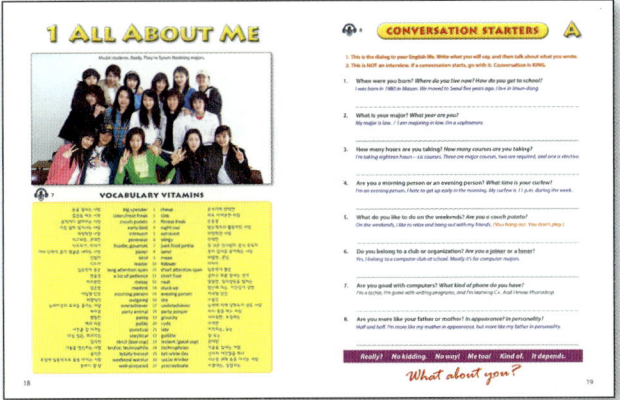

| Top Cultural Differences and vocabulary crossword puzzle | Example paragraph for longer and better speaking | SPEAKING, SPEAKING, SPEAKING
Don't forget to breathe. |

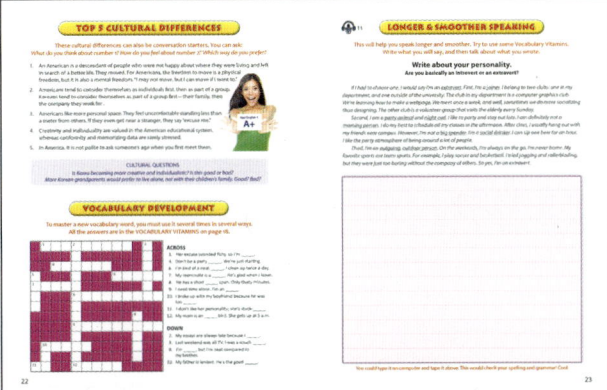

INSTRUCTIONS FOR STUDENTS

DO THE BOOK AT HOME, SPEAK IN CLASS.

Page 1: Listen and pronounce the Vocabulary Vitamins. As you do, highlight some of the words that you like and will use later.

Pages 2 - 3: Listen and pronounce. Then write your own answers, and try to use the new vocabulary. This is the English dialog to your life. Write what you will say, and talk about what you wrote.

Page 4: Listen and pronounce—several times. Record yourself and listen.

Page 5: Read the Cultural Differences. Do the Crossword Puzzle. All the answers to the puzzle are in the Vocabulary Vitamins. This will help integrate the new vocabulary. And it's fun.

Page 6: Listen and pronounce the practice paragraph, and then write your own. This makes your speaking longer and smoother. Write what you will say, and talk about what you wrote.

Pages 7 - 8: Construct sixteen conversation questions. This improves your thinking and speaking. (Conversations require questions.) Then you use the questions in your conversations.

 The icon for the audio files is earphones AND a microphone. Why?
To improve you must listen, repeat, record yourself, and listen to yourself.

5

INSTRUCTIONS FOR TEACHERS

PAGE 1: VOCABULARY VITAMINS

1. Strongly encourage students to bring in family photos. Korean wedding photos contain many family members.

2. Pronounce the vocabulary. Explain where needed or interesting. Make sure students know about the Explanations & Examples section at the back of the book.

3. The unit pretest is multiple-choice listening and covers vocabulary. Therefore, to do well on it, students must listen and know how the new vocabulary is pronounced.

PAGES 2 & 3: CONVERSATION STARTERS

1. Remind students that each question is meant to start a conversation.

2. Remind students to make comments (*Really? Me too! No way!*) and to ask follow-up questions (*Where, When, Why, Who? What about you?*).

3. The questions can be asked in any order the student chooses. However, students should understand and be able to answer all the questions.

4. Both students open the book. One asks page A questions, the other page B. Neither student can read the question they are being asked. This improves their listening.

5. In the third class period, to add variety, students can sit in groups of three. One student uses page A, one uses page B, and one uses the C pages, which are the last two pages of the unit.

SPEED DATING: One interesting topic (me), many partners

1. Students sit in pairs, in straight rows. (If the rows are not straight, switching partners is chaotic.)

2. Every five to ten minutes, yell SWITCH! Remind students to say goodbye and hello: *Later, See you later, Gotta go, Nice to meet you. Hi, my name is Kim Min-soo. I like your hairdo.*

3. In one class, students will switch four to six times. In a class of twenty, they can switch nine times and never have the same partner again. That is three or four weeks without talking to the same person twice. VARIETY! If you explain your hobby nine times, you will surely improve.

4. If students tire of questions, or answers, they simply ask other questions.

5. By repeating common questions and answers, students get a variety of answers and a variety of ways that answers are pronounced.

6. If students' questions or answers are not understood, they can try different pronunciations until they find the one that works.

PAGE 4: MODEL CONVERSATION

1. This page gives students a natural conversation model.
2. Students are urged to listen and pronounce the audio, repeatedly.
3. Teachers can put the students in pairs to practice the dialogues.
4. There is often some kind of checklist to fill out. This is part of the homework check, and it also provides conversation starters.

PAGE 5: TOP CULTURAL DIFFERENCES

1. Teachers can explain these. Perhaps they know of current movies that illustrate some of the differences.
2. The Cultural Differences can also be conversation starters.
3. The crossword puzzles are actually easy fill-in-the-blank vocabulary exercises (because you know exactly how many letters are in the answer). All the answers are in the Vocabulary Vitamins on the first page of each unit.

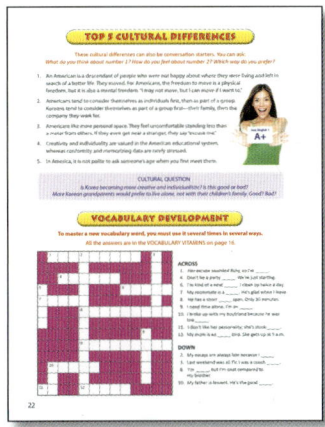

PAGE 6: SPEAKING AMMUNITION

1. Writing helps students speak longer and more smoothly.
2. The model helps them to write well-organized paragraphs.
3. Students should try to use Vocabulary Vitamins in their paragraphs.
4. They are encouraged to listen to the paragraph with the book closed first. Then they open the book and follow along. This improves listening.

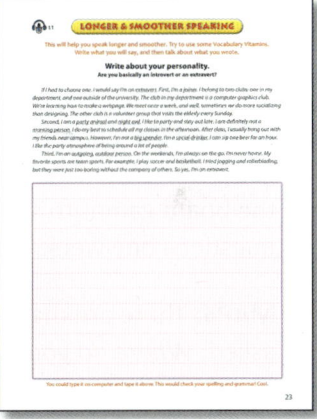

PAGES 7 & 8: CONVERSATION STATION

1. The A and B pages at the beginning of the unit are for pair conversations. Conversation Station can be used as the C page in trio conversations.
2. For homework: At the top of each box is information that students want to get. To get that information, they must form and ask certain questions. For example, if the information is *Find someone's hobby*, students try to create the appropriate question: *"Are you have hobby?"* Then they check below and find that their question is incorrect. They should have used, *"Do you have a hobby?"*
3. In class, students can sit in groups of three. One student uses page A, one uses page B, and one uses these C pages.

DO THE BOOK AT HOME, SPEAK IN CLASS.

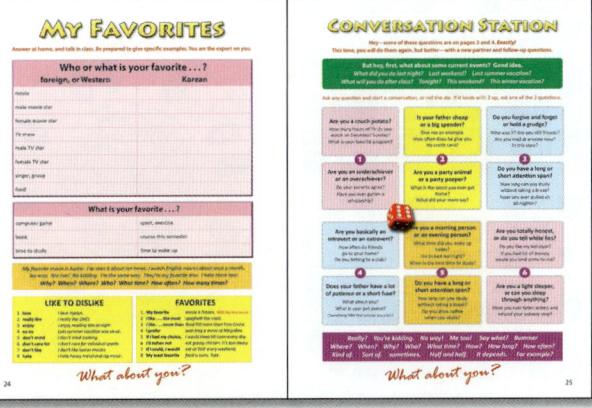

7

SUPPORT UNITS

1. **CORE VOCABULARY**: The vocabulary is translated and can be used to support any unit. When the electricity fails, you can pronounce one of these sheets.

    JOBS, PERSONALITY, and LOOKS are useful in **Unit 1: Family** for talking about family members.

    CLOTHING and LOOKS are good for **Unit 6: Shopping,** and Looks is also good for **Unit 5: Movies**.

2. **DESCRIBING, FREQUENCY, QUALITY, COMPARISON:**
    The DESCRIBING activity is for both males and females. What a hoot!
    In conversation, you also talk about how often you do something (FREQUENCY), how fun or awful it is (QUALITY), and how it is different from something else (COMPARISON).

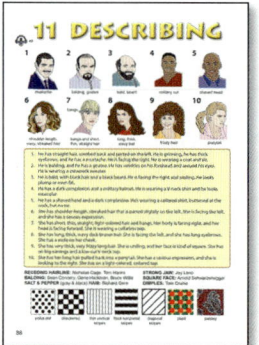   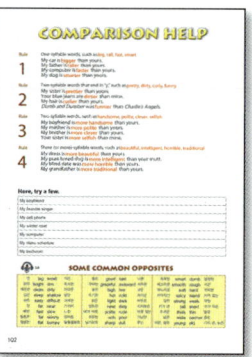

3. **BOARD GAMES:** The board games in back can be used as often as you like. The Free Talking Frenzy game is a great ice-breaker on the first day of class. Later in the semester when interest is flagging, use the board games to spice things up. You could do the Free Talking game systematically: Do the blue questions one week, then the red, then the purple, then the green. Each color has a variety of questions.

4. **MAPS:** There are maps of Seoul, Korea, the USA, and the world. Maps are a great help when you are asked: *Where do you live? How do you get to school? What did you do last summer?*

72 questions in 4 colors
Do a different color every week.

128 Jazz Questions!
I kid you not.

KOREA
Where did you go last summer?

SEOUL
Where do you live?

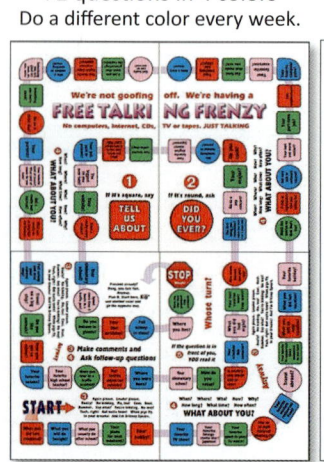  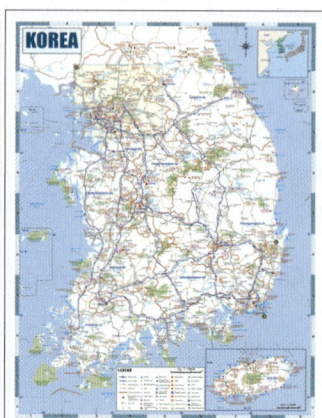 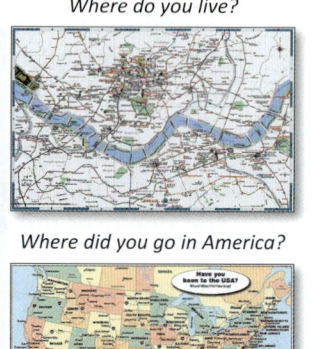

Where did you go in America?

THE CLASS: SPEED DATING

The engine of improvement is SPEED DATING. It provides FOCUS, VARIETY, and REPETITION.

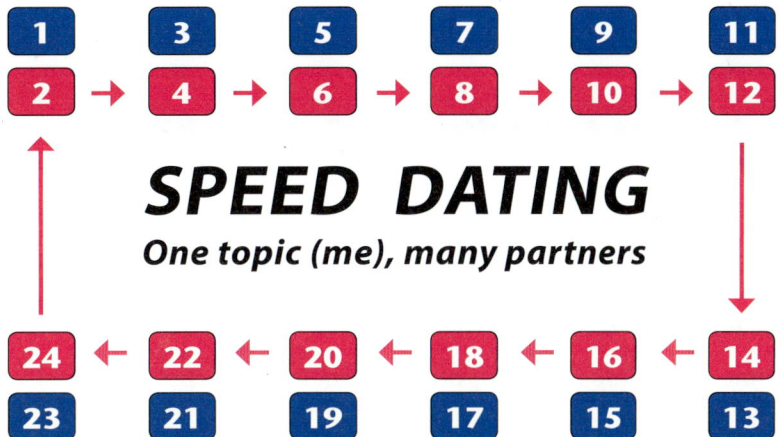

THE BIGGER THE CLASS, THE BETTER.
More partners = more variety = more interesting = more repetition = more improvement

IN BRIEF

1. **Pretest**: Students do the book at home and speak in class. The unit pretests force students to cover the book at home.
2. **First class**: SPEED DATE using the A and B pages. Students master hearing and answering the **BASICS**.
3. **Second class**: Speed date in pairs again, with new partners, getting **SMOOTHER** and **BETTER**.
   Or use the A, B, and C pages—with new partners—for longer trio conversations. **VARIETY**.

1st CLASS
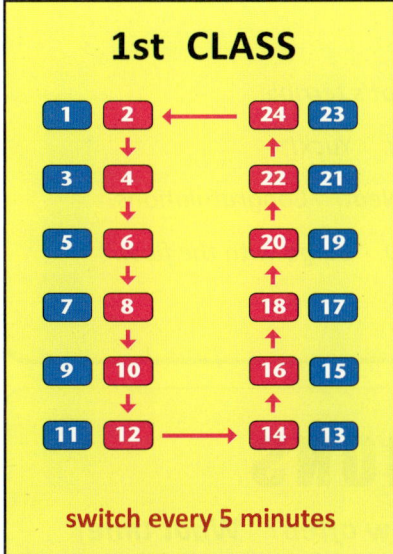
switch every 5 minutes

1. Students sit like so, odds with evens.
2. You yell **SPEAK**.
3. After five minutes, you yell **SWITCH**.
4. Odds stay, evens move.

2nd CLASS
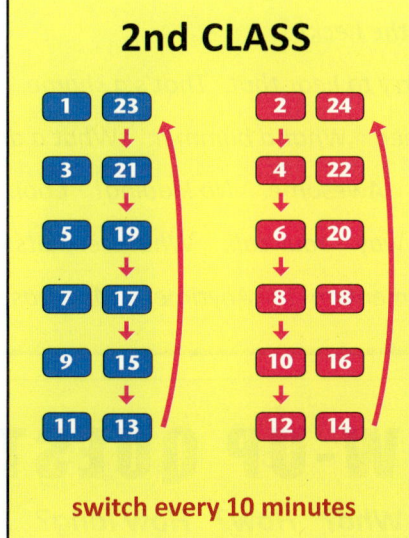
switch every 10 minutes

1. To ensure new partners, odds sit with odds and evens with evens.
2. You yell *Introduce yourself* and **SPEAK!**
3. After ten minutes, you yell **SWITCH!**

3rd CLASS
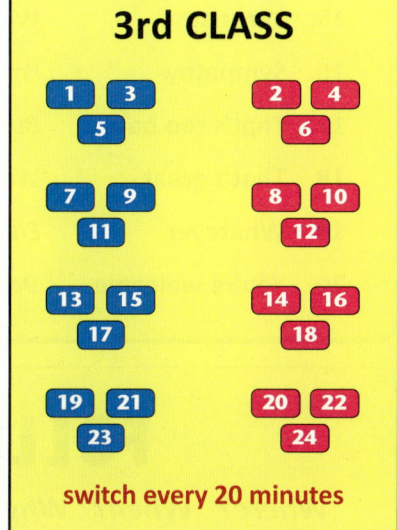
switch every 20 minutes

1. To ensure new partners and add variety, put students in threes.
2. You yell *Introduce yourself* and **SPEAK!**
3. After twenty minutes, you yell **SWITCH!**

REAL-WORLD ENGLISH

You're going to be having a lot of conversations.
Here are real-world comments and follow-up questions that keep conversations going.

TOP 20 COMMENT CATEGORIES

1.	Agree	Me too. I hear that. Ditto. Absolutely. You got that right.
2.	Disagree	No way. Not me. When pigs fly. In your dreams.
3.	Change the topic	Anyway. By the way.
4.	Don't do that	Stop it. Cut it out. Knock it off!
5.	Hurry up	Chop chop. Cut to the chase. Shake a leg.
6.	I don't believe you	You're kidding. No way! Get real. Yeah, right. In your dreams. Say what?
7.	I don't care	Whatever.
8.	I don't understand	Excuse me? Again, please. Say what?
9.	I want to also	I'm game. Count me in.
10.	I'm not sure	I have no idea. I have no clue. I have no earthly idea.
11.	Mistake	My bad. Oops. Uh-oh.
12.	Pain	Ouch! Eye yai yai.
13.	Privacy	No comment. That's personal. That's none of your business.
14.	Sarcasm	Hello? Anybody home?
15.	Surprise	What the heck!
16.	Sympathy	I'm sorry to hear that. That's a shame. That's terrible.
17.	That's too bad	Bummer. What a bummer. What a drag. Yuck!
18.	That's great	Wow! Awesome. No kidding! Cool. Neat. Congratulations.
19.	Whatever	Either way. Your call. Whatever suits you. I'll go with the flow.
20.	You're welcome	Don't mention it. Anytime. My pleasure.

FOLLOW-UP QUESTIONS

Where? When? Why? Who? How? How long? How often? What time?

And the greatest conversation question in the English language:

WHAT ABOUT YOU?

Sample Conversation

There are over 300 conversation-starting questions in this book.
You know the answer to every one because every question is about you.

Today, RIGHT NOW, get in the habit of making comments and asking follow-up questions.
This will make all your conversations longer and more interesting, like you.

Brad	Hi. My name is Brad Kim.
Britney	Hello, my name is Britney Lee. Nice to meet you.
Brad	Nice to meet you too. I got here a little late. Did the professor say anything important?
Britney	Oh, the usual blah blah blah and something about late students getting an F for the day.
Brad	Say what?
Britney	Just kidding. Do you live far from school?
Brad	No, I live within walking distance, about ten minutes away. What about you?
Britney	Me too. Where exactly do you live?
Brad	I live in that new tall apartment complex near Hoegi Station.
Britney	I live in the other direction, near Gwangmyeong. What's your major?
Brad	I'm majoring in economics. What about you?
Britney	My major is business and my minor is English.
Brad	Wow. I've never seen a pen like this. How does it work? Oops. My bad. Is this your homework?
Britney	Not anymore.
Brad	Sorry about that. Anyway, did you come straight to college or did you stay out a year?
Britney	Actually, I stayed out two years.
Brad	No way! Me too. Did you travel or do anything in those two years?
Britney	I lived with my aunt in Canada for a year to improve my English.
Brad	Cool. What does your aunt do?
Britney	She's a housewife. The good news is I spent a year in Canada. The bad news is I spent a lot of time speaking Korean to my aunt's family. What about you? What did you do for two years?
Brad	Well, I tutored some students in math, but their scores didn't improve, so I got fired.
Britney	Bummer.
Brad	Yeah, when they got their scores, I was like, what the heck? But I think maybe they did badly on the test just to get me fired.
Britney	Were they neighborhood kids?
Brad	My little brother and sister.
Britney	No way! Your own mother fired you?
Brad	Absolutely.
Britney	Are you close to your brother and sister?
Brad	Not anymore.

FIRST-DAY SPEED DATING!

But we are total strangers. Exactly!
You'll switch partners every five minutes and meet a new stranger.

Do you have a hobby? (A real hobby?) (Listening to music or watching movies is not a hobby.) How long have you had it? Why do you like it?

Have you ever had a part-time job? What kind of job? Where was it? Did you ever tutor students? How long did you work? Was the money good?

Have you ever missed school because you were sick? Did you go to the hospital? The emergency room? How long did you miss school? Do you ever exercise? Do you play any team sports?

Have you ever told your parents a big lie? What was the lie? Why did you lie? Did you feel guilty afterwards? Did your parents ever find out?

Have you ever won a contest? (music, art, writing, sports, math, whatever) Wow. I'm impressed. When? Where? What kind of prize? Were your parents proud?

Have you ever gone to a pop music concert? When? Where? Who did you go with? Was it indoors or outdoors? What other groups were there? Was it great or just OK?

Describe your favorite movie star. DON'T TELL ME THEIR NAME so I can try to guess. Are they Korean or American? Young or old? What kind of movies are they in?

Have you ever fallen asleep in class? How long ago? What class? How long were you asleep? What did the teacher say?

Say what? Really? No way. Me too! Bummer. Where? When? Why? Who? How?

Have you ever seen a movie star, or music star, or TV star, in person? Where? When? How close did you get to them? Were they better-looking in person? Were they nice or stuck-up?

Have you ever had a really scary dream? What was the dream about? How often do you have scary dreams? Do you remember your dreams?

Which is more fun, high school or college? Why? What do you miss most about high school? What do you like most about college?

How many text messages do you send and get per pay? How many phone calls do you get per day? Do you ever text in class?

What is your favorite computer game? Are you good? Do you play every day? How long do you play? What is the longest you have ever played? Where do you play?

Have you ever gone to a classical music concert? Where? How long ago? What orchestra or performer? Do you play a musical instrument? Are you good?

If you could visit anywhere in the world, where would you go? What countries have you been to? How long were you there? How was it? When did you go?

Have you ever eaten food that made you sick? What was it? Where were you? Did other people get sick also? How long were you sick? Does that happen often?

Do you like animals? Do you have a pet? Have you ever had a pet? What kind? Male or female? How old is it? Do you like going to the zoo?

Do you go to an academy these days? Do you go before or after school? How many days per week? Do you go on Saturday? Have you ever gone to an academy?

Have you ever been punished for coming home late? Why were you late? What was the punishment? Who was angrier, your father or mother?

Have you ever stayed up all night studying? Really? Wow! For what subject? What time did you finally go to sleep? How did you do on the test? Is this your favorite class?

Tell me about your favorite TV show. DO NOT TELL ME THE NAME so I can try to guess. Is it a comedy or drama? What day does it come on? What time? How long does it last? Who is the star?

Have you ever stayed up all night partying? Drinking? Wow. What time did you get home? What is the latest that you ever got home? What did your mom say?

What is the first thing you remember in your whole life (your earliest memory)? How old were you? Why do you think you remember that particular thing?

What is the longest you ever slept non-stop? Studied non-stop? Watched TV non-stop? What was it? Where were you? What time do you usually go to bed? What time do you wake up?

What about you?

Be a rebel. Ask any question. Or use the die. If it lands with 3 up, ask any 3 question.

12

& FOLLOW-UP QUESTION FRENZY

Sit face to face with your partner. Turn your book sideways. Your partner's book is closed.

Meet, greet, introduce yourself, ask any question, make comments, have a conversation, say goodbye.

Have you ever had a broken bone or other serious injury?
What happened? Do you have a scar? Was it painful? Did you get stitches?

What is your zodiac sign?
Do you believe in that zodiac stuff? What is your blood type? Are you the year of the dragon? Year of the snake?

What is the longest you have ever gone without sleeping?
What time do you usually go to bed? What time do you usually wake up? How often do you take a nap?

Tell me about your schedule this semester.
How many hours are you taking? Do you have a free day? What is your busiest day? Do you like your major?

If you could have a front-row seat at any concert of any band, who would it be?
Why? What is your favorite kind of music? Who is your favorite singer or group?

Have you ever gone on a strict diet?
How long were you on the diet? Did it work? What kind of foods did you eat? How much weight did you lose?

What are your pet peeves? (Pet peeves are little things that make you angry; for example, I hate it when people count their money before leaving the ATM.)

What is most important to you in a husband or wife: face, body, money, height, personality?
Do you believe in love at first sight? Tell me about your first crush.

Tell me about your favorite singer. DO NOT TELL ME THEIR NAME so I can try to guess.
Is it a single person or a group? How many people are in the group? What kind of music do they play?

Have you ever traveled abroad?
When? How long were you there? Who did you go with? Did you make any new friends? Which country or place did you like best?

Have you ever fallen asleep and missed your subway station or bus stop?
How long ago? Where? Does that happen often? How did you finally wake up?

Do you believe in ghosts?
Why? Have you ever seen a ghost? What happened? Tell me a scary ghost story. Has a ghost ever stolen your homework? Every week? Amazing.

Have you ever said no when someone asked you out?
Who asked you? Why did you say no?

Have you ever been a class leader?
When? Where? How many times? Did you like it? Did you become a dictator? Are you a people person? Are you a joiner?

Are you close to your brother or sister?
Do you ever argue or fight? Why? What is your age gap? Do you wish you had more siblings, or fewer?

Do you belong to a club or organization?
How long have you belonged? How many members are in the club? How often do you meet? Is it a school club?

What is the most embarrassing thing that has ever happened to you?
Where? How old were you? What did you do after that? How many people saw you?

What was your best vacation or semester break ever?
Why? When? Where? Who were you with? What was your worst vacation or semester break?

Tell me about your favorite movie. DO NOT TELL ME THE NAME so I can try to guess.
What kind of movie is it? Is it a new movie or an old classic?

Are you very good at anything?
Is anyone in your family very talented at something? How long have you been doing that? Tell me more.

Are you good with computers?
What programs do you know? Do you have a printer at home? How many emails do you send and get per day?

If it's not too personal, what is your religion?
Is your whole family the same faith? Do you believe strongly, or so-so? Are you active in your church?

How many other universities did you apply to?
Which ones? Which school was your first choice? Would you like to transfer to another university? Do you like your major? Is this your favorite class?

What is your favorite sport or exercise?
Do you like to exercise? How often do you exercise? What is your favorite sport?

Say what? Really? No way. Me too! Bummer. Where? When? Why? Who? How? *What about you?*

This is not interview class. It's CONVERSATION class. If a conversation starts, go with it. Conversation is KING.

13

CLASSROOM MT

Meeting, Greeting, Inviting Out, Accepting, & Rejecting *Ugh!*

> Introduce yourself to seven people and make a date for every day of the week.
> If they're busy on Friday, ask them about Saturday. If they're busy on Saturday, ask about Sunday.

1. **MEETING:** *Hi/Hey/Hello, my name is . . . How are you? How's it going? I like your hair.* 🎧 3
2. **INVITING:** *What are you doing after class? Are you busy after class? Are you free on Saturday? Are you free Thursday afternoon? Do you have any plans this weekend?*
3. **ACCEPTING:** *OK. Yes. Cool. Great. I'd love to. Let's do it. Sounds like fun. Awesome.*
4. **ARRANGING:** *When are you free? What time are you free? What time is good? Where do you want to meet? Where is convenient? Do you have any place in mind?*
5. **DETAILS:** *Downtown is big; where exactly? By the statue? By Popeye's? In front of TGIF?*
6. **REJECTING** (honestly): *Bummer, I'm busy. I have to work. My uncle asked me to help him move. Can I have a rain check?* = "I really want to go. Ask me again some other time."
7. **REJECTING** (lying): *Oh gee, I'm busy. I have plans. My grandmother is sick. I have to wash my hair.*
8. **SCHEDULING:** *I'm busy today, but Friday I'm free. I'm busy this Saturday, but next Saturday is good. I'm free on Thursday afternoon. What about you? Is Wednesday good? I'm free then.*

Example	Who	Britney Lee	When 4:30	Who		When	Thursday
	Where	Central Plaza fountain		Where			
	Number	017-555-9483		Number			
	Email	breezelee@gmail.com		Email			
Monday	Who		When	Who		When	**Friday**
	Where			Where			
	Number			Number			
	Email			Email			
Tuesday	Who		When	Who		When	**Saturday**
	Where			Where			
	Number			Number			
	Email			Email			
Wednesday	Who		When	Who		When	**Sunday**
	Where			Where			
	Number			Number			
	Email			Email			

This activity will show you how to:

1. Introduce yourself and invite someone out
2. Politely say yes
3. Politely arrange a convenient time
4. Politely say no (honestly, or with a white lie)

MODEL CONVERSATION

Are you a social butterfly?
(very popular, always doing something)

Brad	Hi, my name is Brad Kim.
Britney	Hello, I'm Britney Lee. Nice to meet you.
Brad	Same here.
Britney	I see you have a new iPhone. I just got one, and I'm learning how to use it. Could I buy you a cup of coffee after class so you could show me some things?
Brad	I'd love to, but I have to go to my part-time job. How about tomorrow?
Britney	Heck. Tomorrow I'm busy. I'm meeting with my study group. What about Thursday?
Brad	Thursday after class I play soccer. How about Friday?
Britney	Friday's great. Where and when?
Brad	I finish class at 3:00. What about you?
Britney	Me too. So, how about meeting at 3:15?
Brad	Great. Where?
Britney	How about the Coffee Beaner near the front gate?
Brad	That works. My number is 019-435-6724. And just in case, my email is bradster@gmail.com.
Britney	Got it. My number is 018-784-3412. And my email is brezlee@naver.com.
Brad	Got it. But you know, the iPhone is so easy to learn, by Friday you may not need my help.
Britney	OK. Then never mind.
Brad	But, but . . .
Britney	Just kidding. I had you going. We'll meet, and if nothing else we can talk about this class. The professor is so attractive and funny.
Brad	Sure. Wait, are you talking about THIS class?

This is not reading or writing class. It is conversation class.
DO NOT write your own information down for the other students. YOU say it, and THEY write it. NOBODY reads.

If you have a **D**, **B**, or **P** in your address, he other person may not hear it correctly.
So you might have to say, *D as in dog, B as in boy, P as in puppy.*
The same for **M** and **N**. *Did you say M as in money? No, I said N as in no.*
The same for **Z** and **G**. *Was that Z as in zero or G as in go?*

Do NOT LOOK at their calendar to see if they are free. ASK THEM! This is not reading class.

15

PERSONALITY TEST

What kind of personality do you have?
Are you an exciting party animal, or a studious party pooper?

		Ex.	Me		Ex.	Me
1	Are you a workaholic 일에 중독된 사람	✓		or a slacker? 일하기를 싫어하는 게으른 사람		
2	Are you a morning person 아침에 활동적인 사람	✓		or an evening person? 저녁형 인간		
3	Are you an indoor person 실내에서 활동하기를 좋아하는 사람	✓		or an outdoor person? 밖에서 활동하기 좋아하는 사람		
4	Are you a loner 혼자 있기를 좋아하는 사람	✓		or a joiner? 모임에 가입하거나 참여하기를 좋아하는 사람		
5	Are you neat 깔끔한, 정리정돈 잘하는	✓		or messy? 지저분한		
6	Are you punctual 시간을 잘 지키는	✓		or sometimes late? 가끔 지각하는		
7	Do you have patience 참을성 있는			or a short fuse? 화를 쉽게 잘 내는 사람	✓	
8	Are you a light sleeper 자면서도 인기척을 다 아는 사람			or can you sleep through anything? 죽은듯이 깊게 자는	✓	
9	Are you skeptical 의심이 많은	✓		or gullible? 잘 속는		
10	Are you cheap 인색한	✓		or a big spender? 돈을 잘 쓰는 사람		
11	Are you a moocher 남에게 항상 빌리는 사람	✓		or do you hate to borrow things? 남에게 빌리는 것을 싫어하는		
12	Are you an early bird 아침형 인간	✓		or a night owl? 밤늦게 활동적인 사람		
13	Are you a party pooper 파티를 망치는 사람			or a party animal? 파티를 좋아하는 사람, 파티광	✓	
14	Are you honest 정직한	✓		or do you tell white lies? 선한 거짓말을 하는		
15	Are you a gourmet 미식가	✓		or a junk-food junkie? 패스트푸드 중독자		
16	Do you have a long 집중력이 좋은	✓		or short attention span? 집중력이 짧은	✓	
17	Are you well-organized 정리정돈을 매우 잘하는	✓		or do you often lose things? 자주 물건을 잃어버리는		
18	Do you forgive and forget 화를 쉽게 풀고 잊는 사람			or hold a grudge? 화를 쉽게 풀지 않고 오랫동안 마음속에 품고 있는	✓	
19	Are you a social drinker 사교를 위해 술 마시는 사람	✓		or a weekend warrior? 주말에 집중적으로 술을 마시는 사람		
20	Are you a detail person 꼼꼼하게 하는 사람	✓		or an idea person? 창의적으로 아이디어를 고안하는 사람		

A high total here means you will be rich but a little bit boring. **16**

A high total here means you will be happy but not rich. **5**

Really?   No kidding.   No way!   Say what?   Me too!   Bummer.
Kind of.   Sometimes.   Half and half.   It depends.   Why?   How, exactly?   For example?

What about you?

INSTRUCTIONS

HOMEWORK: 1. Follow the examples. If you are shy, put a check in the box next to *shy*.
2. Add up how many checks you have in each column.

CLASSWORK: 1. Introduce yourself to your partner and give them a personality test.
2. If you are not totally honest, you can use "Kind of" or "It depends."
3. When your partner answers "It depends," ask "How, exactly?" or "For example?"

EXAMPLE CONVERSATION  6

Brad	Hi, my name's Brad.
Britney	Hi, Brad, I'm Britney. Nice to meet you.
Brad	Same here. Say, before we begin, what's your major?
Britney	Same as yours—du-uh. Don't you recognize me from last semester?
Brad	Oh, I'm so sorry. Did you change your hair? You look stunning. Absolutely beautiful.
Britney	Really? Well, thank you so much. Wait. Are you <u>totally honest</u> are do you <u>tell white lies</u>?
Brad	Heh heh heh. Yes, I <u>tell white lies</u> every now and then. And you seem very <u>gullible</u>.
Britney	Very funny. Yes, I am <u>gullible</u>.
Brad	Well, I hope you <u>forgive and forget</u> and don't <u>hold a grudge</u>. I was just trying to loosen things up. The beginning of school can be stressful.
Britney	No way. I much prefer school to the part-time job I had over the summer.
Brad	What did you do?
Britney	I tutored three middle school kids in math. Ugh.
	OK. So, you do have a <u>lot of patience</u> or a <u>short fuse</u>?
Britney	Well, when we began I had a <u>lot of patience</u>, but soon their laziness just got to me. Well, they weren't really lazy. They just had <u>short attention spans</u>.
Brad	But you have a <u>lot of patience</u> with your classmates, right?
Britney	Hurry up and ask the next question!
Brad	Oh, sorry.
Britney	Kidding! You're <u>gullible</u> too.
Brad	You got me. So, are you a <u>morning person</u> or an <u>evening person</u>?
Britney	<u>Half and half</u>. During the week I'm a morning person, and on the weekends I'm an evening person. I have first-period classes on Monday, Wednesday, and Friday.
Brad	<u>Bummer</u>. I'm totally a <u>morning person</u>. I cannot concentrate after sundown. If I don't do my homework in the morning, I never do it.
Britney	Well, if you're a <u>morning person</u>, then why were you always late for class last semester?
Brad	Oh, this is the new me! I'm going to focus, make straight As, and get a scholarship this semester.
Britney	Wow. You really have a good sense of humor! This class will be fun.
Brad	I was serious about getting a scholarship.
Britney	Yeah, right, and I'm Hyolyn.

This activity only *pretends* to be an interview. If a conversation starts, go with it.

1 All About Me

Scan and find the tracks.

Model students. Really. They're Sports Modeling majors.

 7

VOCABULARY VITAMINS

Personality Opposites

big spender	돈을 잘쓰는 사람	cheap	돈 쓰기에 인색한
clean/neat freak	깔끔을 떠는 사람	slob	매우 지저분한 사람
couch potato	움직이기 싫어하는 사람	fitness freak	운동광
early bird	아침 일찍 일어나는 사람	night owl	밤늦게까지 활동적인 사람
introvert	내성적인 사람	extravert	외향적인 사람
generous	너그러운, 관대한	stingy	인색한
foodie; gourmet	식도락가, 미식가	junk food junkie	질 낮은 인스턴트 음식 중독자
joiner	여러 단체에 즐겨 얼굴을 내미는 사람	loner	혼자 있기를 좋아하는 사람
kind	친절한	mean	비열한, 못된
leader	지도자	follower	지지자
long attention span	집중력이 좋은	short attention span	집중력이 짧은
a lot of patience	참을성	short fuse	급하고 화를 잘내는 성격
messy	지저분한	neat	깔끔한, 정리정돈을 잘하는
modest	겸손한	stuck-up	잘난 체 하는, 자만심이 강한
morning person	아침형 인간	evening person	저녁형 인간
outgoing	외향적인	shy	수줍은
overachiever	능력 이상의 효과를 올리는 사람	underachiever	능력에 비해 성취도가 낮은 사람
party animal	파티광	party pooper	파티 흥을 깨는 사람
perky	활발한	grouchy	시무룩한, 투덜대는
polite	예의 바른	rude	무례한
punctual	시간을 잘 지키는	late	지각하는, 늦는
skeptical	의심 많은, 회의적인	gullible	잘 속는
strict (bad cop)	엄격한	lenient (good cop)	관대한
techie; technophile	기술을 맹신하는 사람	technophobe	기술을 겁내는 사람
totally honest	솔직한	tell white lies	선의의 거짓말을 하다
weekend warrior	주말에 집중적으로 술을 마시는 사람	social drinker	사교를 위해 술을 마시는 사람
well-prepared	준비가 잘 된	procrastinate	꾸물대는, 질질끄는

CONVERSATION STARTERS

1. This is the dialog to your English life. Write what you will say, and then talk about what you wrote.
2. This is NOT an interview. If a conversation starts, go with it. Conversation is KING.

1. **When were you born?** *Where do you live now? How do you get to school?*
   I was born in 1990 in Masan. We moved to Seoul five years ago. I live in Imun-dong.

   _____

2. **What is your major?** *What year are you?*
   My major is law. / I am majoring in law. I'm a sophomore.

   _____

3. **How many hours are you taking?** *How many courses are you taking?*
   I'm taking eighteen hours—six courses. Three are major courses, two are required, and one is elective.

   _____

4. **Are you a morning person or an evening person?** *What time is your curfew?*
   I'm an evening person. I hate to get up early in the morning. My curfew is 11 p.m. during the week.

   _____

5. **What do you like to do on the weekends?** *Are you a couch potato?*
   On the weekends, I like to relax and hang out with my friends. (**You hang out. You don't play.**)

   _____

6. **Do you belong to a club or organization?** *Are you a joiner or a loner?*
   Yes, I belong to a computer club at school. Mostly it's for computer majors.

   _____

7. **Are you good with computers?** *What kind of phone do you have?*
   I'm a techie. I'm good with writing programs, and I'm learning C+. And I know Photoshop.

   _____

8. **Are you more like your father or mother?** *In appearance? In personality?*
   Half and half. I'm more like my mother in appearance, but more like my father in personality.

   _____

| Really? | No kidding. | No way! | Me too! | Kind of. | It depends. |

What about you?

CONVERSATION STARTERS  9

This is the dialog to your English life. Write what you will say, and talk about what you wrote.

9. **What did you do last weekend?** *What will you do this weekend?*
   Last weekend, I went shopping for new clothes for school. I'm going for a cool, new look.
   _____

10. **What did you do last summer?** *Have you ever traveled abroad?* **(NOT** *to abroad***)**
    Last summer I went to Jeju for a week with some classmates. I went to Canada once.
    _____

11. **Are you close to your grandparents?** *Any of your aunts, uncles, cousins?*
    I am close to my maternal grandmother. She used to babysit me when I was young.
    _____

12. **How many times has your family moved?** *Which is your favorite place? Why?*
    We've moved only once. I was born in Anyang, and we moved to Seoul when I was 10.
    _____

13. **Are you very talented in something—sports, music, art, math?** *Is anyone in your family?*
    I have a fifth-degree black belt in taekwondo. I belong to the club here at school.
    _____

14. **What does your father do?** *Does your mother work?*
    My father is a high-school math teacher, and my mother used to be a nurse but isn't anymore.
    _____

15. **Who is stricter, your father or mother?** *What was your worst punishment ever?*
    It depends. My father is stricter about grades, and my mother is stricter about curfew.
    _____

16. **Do you have a part-time job? Have you ever?** *Do your parents give you an allowance?*
    I had a part-time job as a waitress at a coffee shop last winter. And I tutor a student in math.
    _____

Write your own question: *Have you ever seen a movie star in person?*

| Where? | When? | Who? | Why? | How? | How long? | How often? |

What about you?

MODEL CONVERSATION

Brad   *Hi. My name is Brad Kim.*

Britney   *Hi. My name is Britney Lee. Nice to meet you.*

Brad   *Nice to meet you too. Say, do you have a twin sister?*

Britney   *No. Why do you ask?*

Brad   *You look familiar, that's all. Last semester, I had a class with a girl who looks just like you.*

Britney   *Really? Well, I have a lot of first cousins, but none of them go to this school. Was she as pretty as me?*

Brad   *Oh, no. You are much more beautiful than her.*

Britney   *Thank you so much. What's your major?*

Brad   *Diplomacy.*

Britney   *Ha. Now I get it. Do you always tell white lies?*

Brad   *Only on the first day of class. Enjoy it while it lasts. What's your major?*

Britney   *Acting. And that <u>was</u> my twin sister!*

Brad   *Ah. You got me. How is your sister doing?*

Britney   *I was kidding about my twin sister. Is that great acting or what?*

Brad   *Anyway. Are you basically an introvert or an extravert? I'm going to guess extravert.*

Britney   *Yes, I like hanging out with people. What about you?*

Brad   *Half and half. I like hanging out with people, but I also like my time alone. People can bring joy to your life, but they can also bring problems.*

Britney   *I know what you mean. What did you do last summer?*

Brad   *I had a part-time job at Family Mart. Actually, my twin brother and I took turns going to work.*

Britney   *You have a twin brother?*

Brad   *Gotcha!*

Shy guy. Not.

This list can start a conversation also, so be sure to fill it in.

Who is the _____ in your family?
smartest
most talented
best-looking
most outgoing
biggest spender
biggest drinker
cheapest
first to wake up
last to go to bed
biggest TV watcher

Loner

Short attention span

TOP 5 CULTURAL DIFFERENCES

These cultural differences can also be conversation starters. You can ask:
What do you think about number 1? How do you feel about number 2? Which way do you prefer?

1. An American is a descendant of people who were not happy about where they were living and left in search of a better life. They moved. For Americans, the freedom to move is a physical freedom, but it is also a mental freedom. "I may not move, but I can move if I want to."

2. Americans tend to consider themselves as individuals first, then as part of a group. Koreans tend to consider themselves as part of a group first—their family, then the company they work for.

3. Americans like more personal space. They feel uncomfortable standing less than a meter from others. If they even get near a stranger, they say "excuse me."

4. Creativity and individuality are valued in the American educational system, whereas conformity and memorizing data are rarely stressed.

5. In America, it is not polite to ask someone's age when you first meet them.

CULTURAL QUESTIONS
*Is Korea becoming more creative and individualistic? Is this good or bad?
More Korean grandparents would prefer to live alone, not with their children's family. Good? Bad?*

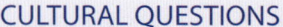

VOCABULARY DEVELOPMENT

To master a new vocabulary word, you must use it several times in several ways.
All the answers are in the VOCABULARY VITAMINS on page 18.

ACROSS
1. Her excuse sounded fishy, so I'm _____.
4. Don't be a party _____. We're just starting.
6. I'm kind of a neat _____. I clean up twice a day.
7. My roommate is a _____. He's glad when I leave.
8. He has a short _____ span. Only thirty minutes.
9. I need time alone. I'm an _____.
10. I broke up with my boyfriend because he was too _____.
11. I don't like her personality; she's stuck-_____.
12. My mom is an _____ bird. She gets up at 5 a.m.

DOWN
2. My essays are always late because I _____.
3. Last weekend was all TV. I was a couch _____.
8. I'm _____, but I'm neat compared to my brother.
10. My father is lenient. He's the good _____.

LONGER & SMOOTHER SPEAKING

This will help you speak longer and smoother. Try to use some Vocabulary Vitamins. Write what you will say, and then talk about what you wrote.

Write about your personality.
Are you basically an introvert or an extravert?

If I had to choose one, I would say I'm an <u>extravert</u>. First, I'm a <u>joiner</u>. I belong to two clubs: one in my department, and one outside of the university. The club in my department is a computer graphics club. We're learning how to make a webpage. We meet once a week, and well, sometimes we do more socializing than designing. The other club is a volunteer group that visits the elderly every Sunday.

Second, I am a <u>party animal</u> and <u>night owl</u>. I like to party and stay out late. I am definitely not a <u>morning person</u>. I do my best to schedule all my classes in the afternoon. After class, I usually hang out with my friends near campus. However, I'm not a <u>big spender</u>. I'm a <u>social drinker</u>. I can sip one beer for an hour. I like the party atmosphere of being around a lot of people.

Third, I'm an <u>outgoing</u>, <u>outdoor person</u>. On the weekends, I'm always on the go. I'm never home. My favorite sports are team sports. For example, I play soccer and basketball. I tried jogging and rollerblading, but they were just too boring without the company of others. So yes, I'm an extravert.

You could type it on computer and tape it above. This would check your spelling and grammar! Cool.

MY FAVORITES

Answer at home, and talk in class. Be prepared to give specific examples. You are the expert on you.

Who or what is your favorite . . . ?	
foreign	**Korean**
movie	
male movie star	
female movie star	
TV show	
male TV star	
female TV star	
singer, group	
food	

What is your favorite . . . ?	
computer game	sport or exercise
book	course this semester
time to study	time to wake up

My favorite movie is Avatar. I've seen it about ten times. I watch English movies about once a month. No way. Me too! No kidding. I'm the same way. They're my favorite also. I hate them too!
Why? When? Where? Who? What time? How often? How many times?

LIKE TO DISLIKE
1. **love** — I love Hyolyn.
2. **really like** — I really like 2NE1.
3. **enjoy** — I enjoy reading late at night.
4. **so-so** — Last summer vacation was so-so.
5. **don't mind** — I don't mind cooking.
6. **don't care for** — I don't care for individual sports.
7. **don't like** — I don't like horror movies.
8. **hate** — I hate heavy metal and rap music.

FAVORITES
1. **My favorite** — movie is Frozen. (NOT *My best movie*)
2. **I like . . . the most** — spaghetti the most.
3. **I like . . . more than** — Brad Pitt more than Tom Cruise.
4. **I prefer** — watching a move at MegaBox.
5. **If I had my choice,** — I would sleep till noon every day.
6. **I'd rather not** — eat greasy chicken. It's too messy.
7. **If I could, I would** — eat at TGIF every weekend.
8. **My least favorite** — food is curry. Yuck.

What about you?

CONVERSATION STATION

Hey—some of these questions are on pages 3 and 4. *Exactly!*
This time, you will do them again, but better—with a new partner and follow-up questions.

> But hey, first, what about some current events? Good idea.
> What did you do last night?   Last weekend?   Last summer vacation?
> What will you do after class?   Tonight?   This weekend?   This winter vacation?

Ask any question and start a conversation, or roll the die. If it lands with 2 up, ask one of the 2 questions.

1
Are you a couch potato?
How many hours of TV do you watch on Saturday? Sunday? What is your favorite show?

Are you an underachiever or an overachiever?
Do your parents agree?
Have you ever gotten a scholarship?

2
Is your father cheap or a big spender?
Give me an example.
How often does he give you his credit card?

Are you a party animal or a party pooper?
What is the latest you ever got home?
What did your mom say?

3
Do you forgive and forget or hold a grudge?
Who was it? Are you still friends?
Are you mad at anyone now?
In this class?

Do you have a long or short attention span?
How long can you study without taking a break?
Have you ever pulled an all-nighter?

4
Are you basically an introvert or an extrovert?
How often do friends go to your home?
Do you belong to a club?

Does your father have a lot of patience or a short fuse?
What about you?
What is your pet peeve?
(something little that annoys you a lot)

5
Are you a morning person or an evening person?
What time did you wake up today?
Go to bed last night?
When is the best time to study?

Do you have a long or short attention span?
How long can you study without taking a break?
Do you drink coffee when you study?

6
Are you totally honest, or do you tell white lies?
Do you like my hairstyle?
If you had lot of money, would you lend some to me?

Are you a light sleeper, or can you sleep through anything?
Have you ever fallen asleep and missed your subway stop?

> Really?   You're kidding.   No way!   Me too!   Say what?   Bummer.
> Where?   When?   Why?   Who?   What time?   How?   How long?   How often?
> Kind of.   Sort of.   sometimes.   Half and half.   It depends.   For example?

What about you?

25

2 WEEKENDS & NEIGHBORHOODS

Scan and find the tracks.

 12

Vocabulary Vitamins

WEEKEND WORDS		**MOODY TERMS**	
catch up on	부족한 것을 만회하는	anxious	걱정되는, 불안한
fall behind	뒤처지는; 일이 늦어진	cranky; grouchy	짜증내는; 지루퉁한
hang out (NOT play)	친구들과 놀러 다니다	depressed	우울한, 낙담한
look forward to	고대하다	have (got) the blues	우울한; 의기소침한
performance	공연	pout	토라진
quality time	편하고 의미 있는 시간	**TIRED TERMS**	
rewarding	보람 있는	burned out	매우 지친, 몹시 피곤한
tentative plans	임시적인 계획	drained; exhausted	녹초가 된
RELAXING TERMS		sick and tired	반복적인 일에 질린
chill, chill out	진정하는	stressed	스트레스
goof off	빈둥되는	**SLEEPING TERMS**	
kick back	편하게 쉬는	catch some Z's	잠자다
R&R (rest and relaxation)	휴가와 휴양	crash	곯아떨어지다
recharge my batteries	재충전하는	dead to the world	죽은듯이 깊게 자는
take it easy	한가하게 지내는	nap	낮잠
unwind	긴장을 푸는	play possum	자는 척하는

Personality Opposites

always on the go; never home	항상 밖으로 쏘다니는	homebody	집에 있기는 좋아하는
indoors person	내향적인 사람	outdoors person	외향적인 사람
light sleeper	설 잠을 자는, 금방 잘 깨는	sleep through anything	잠을 항상 깊게 자는 사람
party animal	파티를 매우 좋아하는	party pooper	파티 분위기 망치는
spontaneous	충동적인	need advance notice	사전에 미리 알아야 하는
weekend warrior	주말에 술을 매우 많이 마시는	social drinker / teetotaler	조금씩 즐기는 / 절대 금주

 13

CONVERSATION STARTERS

1. This is the dialog to your English life. Write what you will say, and talk about what you wrote.
2. This is NOT an interview. If a conversation starts, go with it. Conversation is KING.

1. **What did you do last weekend?** *What do you usually do?*
   Last weekend, I just took it easy and recharged my batteries. I was burned out from midterm exams.

   _____

2. **Are you an indoor person or an outdoor person?** *Are you an introvert or an extravert?*
   I'm probably more of an indoor person. I could spend hours on the Internet or watching TV.

   _____

3. **Do you use weekends to recharge your batteries or to catch up on schoolwork?**
   Both. Saturdays I try to relax, and Sunday afternoons I try to catch up and prepare for the week.

   _____

4. **What weekend chore do you hate the most?** *Do you ever cook? Do the dishes?*
   I hate cleaning the house, especially the bathroom. Doing the laundry is next.

   _____

5. **Do your parents like your friends?** *Do your friends ever hang out at your home?*
   Frankly, my mom thinks my friends are kind of annoying. They're too spontaneous. They never plan ahead.

   _____

6. **Do you have a hobby?** *Are you skilled at anything? Music, sports, art, science?*
   I guess you could say physical fitness. I've run five marathons, and I belong to a health club.

   _____

7. **Do you ever watch TV for more than five hours straight?** *What's your favorite TV show?*
   Oh, yeah. Some Saturdays, I watch TV from evening to early morning. With naps.

   _____

8. **Do you usually eat out on weekends?** *Do you get food delivered? What kind?*
   When the weather is cool, we like to sit outside and have fried chicken and draft beer.

   _____

| *Really?* | *No kidding.* | *No way!* | *Me too!* | *Bummer.* | *Anyway.* |
| Where? | When? | Why? | Who? | How? | What time? | How often? |

What about you?

CONVERSATION STARTERS

This is the dialog to your English life. Write what you will say, and talk about what you wrote.

9. **Is your neighborhood safe?** *Convenient? Do you live near a river, mountain, or park?*
   My neighborhood is nice. I live in Wangsimni, and that's near Hanyang University and the Han River.
   _____

10. **Do you live in a high-rise?** *Do you know any of your neighbors?*
    I live in a high-rise with my older sister. It has a great view of Seoul Forest.
    _____

11. **Do you have a curfew?** *What time do you usually wake up and go to bed?*
    I used to have a curfew but not anymore. I wake up at 6 during the week and sleep till 10 on the weekends.
    _____

12. **Is your father handy around the house?** *Can he fix things?*
    My father is pretty handy. Last year he put a ceiling fan in every room of the apartment.
    _____

13. **Do you do your homework over the weekends?** (Not Monday morning.)
    I usually start doing my homework on Saturday morning until my attention span runs out.
    _____

14. **Do you ever go to concerts, musicals, or professional baseball games?**
    I went to a few concerts a while back, and I've seen Cats *and* Nanta.
    _____

15. **What do you usually do on Sundays?** *Do you see your grandparents or other relatives?*
    I always do something. I cannot sit still for more than five minutes. On weekends, I'm always on the go.
    _____

16. **Which is your big night, Friday or Saturday?** *How much do you usually spend?*
    Friday night is my big night. I party around school and take the last subway home at midnight.
    _____

Write your own question: ___*Do you hang out near home or school?*___

| Really? | No kidding. | No way! | Me too! | Bummer. | Anyway. |
| Where? | When? | Why? | Who? | How? | What time? | How often? |

What about you?

 15

MODEL CONVERSATION

Brad   Hey, Britney, how was your weekend? Did you do something special?

Britney   No. I just stayed home and <u>recharged my batteries</u>. I was <u>drained</u> from studying for midterms.

Brad   Is that what all those tests were? Midterm exams?

Britney   Say what?

Brad   Just kidding. I'm like you. I was <u>burned out</u> from all those tests. I'm really <u>looking forward to</u> no tests for a while. Do you have any plans for this coming weekend?

Britney   Nothing special. I just hope to have some <u>quality family time</u>. My sister and I have been studying, and my father has been working late. So hopefully, we can all just <u>hang out</u> at home this weekend. What about you?

My top 3 things to do on the weekend
1 sleep
2
3
My last thing to do on the weekend
10 clean the bathroom

Brad   I have <u>tentative plans</u> to go phone shopping with Jack, but we're not exactly sure when or where yet. Frankly, I wouldn't mind just staying home and <u>crashing</u> for the whole weekend.

Britney   I know what you mean. By the time Sunday evening comes around, I start to <u>dread</u> another week of school.

Brad   Well, let's do something different this weekend. Do you want to go white-water rafting?

Britney   This weekend? I'm not <u>spontaneous</u> like you. I <u>need advance notice</u>.

Brad   Oh, come on. You can do it!

Britney   Thanks but no thanks. I would have to buy a whole new outfit. But if you're into water, there's a lake near my grandparents' house where we could rent a boat and paddle around.

Brad   You say <u>we</u> could paddle. You will paddle also?

Britney   Aw, come on, Brad. Man up. You can paddle a small boat by yourself.

Brad   OK, but I don't want to paddle too fast for you. Maybe you should bring some seasickness pills.

Britney   Yeah. I'll bring a whole bottle just in case.

TOP 4 CULTURAL DIFFERENCES

These cultural differences can also be conversation starters. You can ask:
What do you think about number 1? How do you feel about number 2? Which way do you prefer?

1. On Sundays, many Americans watch sports, whereas Koreans watch celebrity games and reality TV shows.
2. Americans are probably a bit more do-it-yourself than Koreans. The average American husband usually has a whole bunch of tools that he uses to fix things around the house. These can be minor things like fixing a toilet or major things like repairing the roof.
3. The average American family has a house with a yard, so mowing the grass and house upkeep and repair are a bigger part of an American's weekend.
4. Sunday is the most common day for American families to get together. Parents and kids often have Sunday dinner with one or both sets of grandparents.

Is your neighborhood . . .	
safe?	✓
quiet?	
fun to spend time in?	
fairly free of traffic?	
convenient for subway, bus?	
convenient for shopping?	
near a park, mountain, river?	
TOTAL	

CULTURAL QUESTIONS
Is Korea becoming more creative and individualistic? Is this good or bad?
More Korean grandparents would prefer to live alone, not with their children's family. Good? Bad?

VOCABULARY DEVELOPMENT

ACROSS
4. You're taking a _____? Wake up and study!
6. Last weekend I stayed home and _____ my batteries.
9. Me too. I goofed _____ all weekend.
10. You bet I'm _____! I'm game for anything, any time.
14. It was great. I had some _____ time with my father.
15. His girlfriend dumped him. He's got the _____.

DOWN
1. I'll _____ up on my studies this weekend. Really.
2. I'm _____ out from midterm tests. I need a break.
3. My mother is a light _____. Bummer.
5. She's a _____. She's never tasted alcohol. Ever.
7. I played _____ and so my mother did the dishes.
8. I have _____ plans to go see my grandparents.
11. I stayed home all weekend and took it _____.
12. I'm bored. Let's go _____ out in Hongdae.
13. I'm _____ and tired of your bad grades and lazy attitude. Shape up or ship out.

 16

LONGER & SMOOTHER SPEAKING

This will help you speak longer and smoother. Try to use some Vocabulary Vitamins.
Write what you will say, and then talk about what you wrote.

Write about your weekends or your neighborhood.
Or write about both. Or write about a hobby that you do on the weekends.

On Fridays after school, I don't <u>hang out</u> around campus; I hurry home. I live in a big high-rise complex in Incheon, and there is lots to do near my home. My <u>commute</u> on the subway to school is about three hours each day, and by Friday night I am <u>exhausted</u>. Luckily, the complex is right next to the subway. My social life is mainly with my high school friends in my neighborhood. I haven't made any university friends yet.

Saturday is my big day. When I hear my mother start to clean the house, I play possum so she won't ask me to help. Then I surf the Internet and <u>catch up on</u> the news. I like to keep up with the latest movie and TV star gossip. Saturday evening I meet my friends, and we usually see a movie and then go to eat kalbi or haemul pajeon. I have no curfew, but I usually get home before midnight.

On Sunday morning, we go pick up my grandmother and go to church. Then my dad takes us out to eat Sunday brunch. Then it's back home, and I watch TV for about six hours straight. If I've fallen behind on my schoolwork, I <u>catch up on</u> that late Sunday night. So on the weekends I get to <u>hang out with</u> my friends, have <u>quality time</u> with my family, and <u>recharge my batteries</u> for the next week of school.

You could type it on computer and tape it above. This would check your spelling and grammar! Cool.

Conversation Station

There are three ways to play:
1. Roll the die, and if it lands with 2 facing up, ask any 2 question.
2. Ask a 1 question, then after everyone answers, ask a 2 question. Then a 3, 4, 5, and 6.
3. Ask the first 1 question, then the second, then the third, then the fourth.

But first, current events! If you are meeting someone for the first time, take care of the basics:
Hi. My name is. . . . Where do you live? What's your major? What high school did you go to?

Do you . . .
1. Cram or prepare ahead of time?
2. Procrastinate until the last minute?
3. Tell white lies often?
4. Hang out near school or your home?

Are you . . .
1. A party animal or party pooper?
2. A weekend warrior or social drinker?
3. A morning person or evening person?
4. Spontaneous or a planner?

Do you ever . . .
1. Cook for the whole family?
2. Clean the whole house?
3. Play possum to avoid cleaning?
4. Do nothing all weekend?

Is your . . .
1. Mother a clean freak? A light sleeper?
2. Father a big spender or cheap?
3. Mother the good cop or bad cop?
4. Father modern or traditional?

What time . . .
1. Do you usually wake up? Go to bed?
2. Do you wake up on Saturday? Sunday?
3. Is your best time to study?
4. Do you go to bed on Saturday night?

When was the last time you . . .
1. Had quality time with your mother?
2. Had quality time with your father?
3. Cleaned the whole house?
4. Cooked? For your whole family?

 Remember, conversation is KING. If a conversation starts, go with it.

Really?   You're kidding.   No kidding?   No way!   Say what?   Bummer.   Me too!
Where?   When?   Why?   Who?   What time?   How?   How long?   How often?
Kind of.   Sort of.   Sometimes.   Half and half.   It depends.   For example?

What about you?

WEEKEND FREQUENCY

HOMEWORK: Fill in the blanks with your answers. For example, look at question 1. If you see your maternal grandparents once a week, write 7. Then put the total below.

CLASSWORK: You and your partner will interview each other. When you answer, try to use a phrase in regular type and a *phrase in italics*. But if a conversation starts, go with it.

Britney	How often do you clean your room?
Brad	Pretty often, about once a month.
Britney	Once a month? That's not pretty often. That's every now and then.
Brad	Well, my mother cleans my room twice a week. How is that?
Britney	Better.
Brad	How often do you clean your room?
Britney	Never. My roommate is a neat freak. She cleans it twice a day.
Brad	Awesome.

If you do something often, it's important to you.
So *How often do you . . . ?* is a great question for finding out what's important to your partner.

Use the die, or not.

HOW OFTEN DO YOU . . . ?

#	Question			#	Question		
1	See your maternal grandparents?	7			Sleep till noon on Saturday?	10	
2	See your paternal grandparents?	1			Sleep till noon on Sunday?	10	
3	Clean your room?	4			Play a computer game?	8	
4	Clean the whole house?	1			Surf the Internet?	7	
5	Exercise or go to a health club?	8			Never do any homework all weekend?	5	
6	Go hiking?	2			Get home after sunrise?	7	
7	Go to the library to study?	5			Illegally download a movie?	8	
8	Study on Saturday AND Sunday?	1			Do your homework on Monday morning?	7	
9	Go to a ball game? (Soccer, baseball)	6			Check your text messages?	9	
10	Go to a movie?	8			Change the TV channel?	6	
11	Cook?	4			Check your email?	10	
12	See a play, concert, or performance?	2			Meet your friends in your neighborhood?	4	
	Total	49			Total	91	

Yipes!

What about you?

1	2	3	4	5
never, never ever	hardly ever	rarely, very seldom	not too often	every now and then
when pigs fly	*once a year*	*twice a year*	*every other month*	*once a month*

6	7	8	9	10
sometimes	usually, generally	frequently, often	every chance I get	all the time
twice a month	*once a week*	*twice a week*	*three times a week*	*100 times a day*

Really? No kidding?	Say what? No way.	Me too. Same here.	Where? When?
Wow. Great. Cool.	In your dreams.	Ditto.	Who? Why?
Awesome.	You're pulling my leg.	My father also.	What time?

33

3 TECHNOLOGY

"Hurry back! I can't understand their English."

 17

VOCABULARY VITAMINS

PERSONALITY OPPOSITES

bargain shopper	할인가격 물건만 사는 사람	impulse buyer / shopper	충동구매자
frugal; thrifty; cheap	알뜰한, 알뜰한, 인색한	big spender	돈을 잘쓰는
gullible	잘 속는	skeptical	의심이 많은
instant gratification	사고 싶은 것을 즉시 사야 하는	delayed gratification	사고 싶은 것을 기다렸다 사는
technophile	신기술에 열광하는 사람	technophobe	신기술에 거부감을 느끼는 사람

TECH TERMS

					PROGRAMS
apps	go viral	memory card	phishing	surf	Word
blogs	GPS	memory stick	RAM	text message	Excel
browser	hacker	monitor	reboot	Twitter	Photoshop
crash	icon	mouse	remote control	universal	Illustrator
data	ID / password	MP3	scan, scanner	USB	Flash
digital camera	iPad, iPhone, iMac	multi-tasking	screen saver	video chat	Acrobat
digital SLR	keyboard	navigation	search engine	virus	PowerPoint
download	laser / inkjet printer	netbook	selfie	voice recognition	Prezi
email	log in / out	netiquette	snail mail	webcam	Skype
flash drive	media player	netizen	SNS	website	Twitter
gadget	megapixel	notebook; laptop	spam	Wi-Fi	

If you don't know what a term means, ask your partner. If they don't know, talk about global warming.

CONVERSATION STARTERS

Write what you will say, and then talk about what you wrote.

1. **What kind of phone do you have?** *Which do you do more, talk or text?*
   I have a brand-new iPhone. I got it this week. It's awesome. I use it for texting and entertainment.

   _____

2. **What kind of computer do you have at home?** *Do you have a printer at home?*
   I have a big iMac desktop at home and a wireless all-in-one. I like a big monitor so I can see clearly.

   _____

3. **Who's better at technology, you or your father?** *Does he have a separate phone for work?*
   My father is very high tech. He only gets top-end tech stuff. Yes, he has a separate company phone.

   _____

4. **Is your mother tech-savvy?** *Does your mother work? Do you call her when you'll be late?*
   My mother is not very tech-savvy. I help her shop, do banking, and get airline tickets—stuff like that.

   _____

5. **How many phones have you had?** *How many have you lost?*
   Let's see. I've had three smart phones and lost two. Well, one was stolen.

   _____

6. **At home, do you spend more time in front of the TV or the computer?**
   I have to be honest. I like watching TV. I was never into computer games. I'm a low-tech couch potato.

   _____

7. **Do you belong to Facebook?** *How much time do you spend on it per week?*
   I have a Facebook page. I used to spend a lot of time there, but not anymore.

   _____

8. **Do you prefer to shop online or in stores?** *What is the last thing you bought?*
   I prefer shopping online—easy, big selection, low prices. And you can read reviews before you buy.

   _____

Really?	*No kidding?*	*No way!*	*Me too!*	*Bummer.*	*Anyway.*
Kind of.	*Half and half.*	*Sometimes.*	*It depends.*	*For example?*	
Where?	*When?*	*Why?*	*Who?*	*How?*	*What time?*	*How often?*

What about you?

 19

CONVERSATION STARTERS

9. **How many text messages to you send and get per day?** *To whom, mainly?*
   I get about 200 messages per day. My boyfriend and I have a running conversation all day long.

   _____

10. **What is your most important tech device?** *Why? Do you want an iPad or tablet?*
    My big iMac. I don't use phones that much. I prefer face-to-face communication. I want an iPad next.

    _____

11. **What computer programs do you know?** *What programs do you want to be better at?*
    I know the basics: Word and Excel. And last summer break, I took a course on Photoshop.

    _____

12. **How often do you download movies?** *Legally? Do you ever file-share?*
    Sometimes I'll download a movie and watch it when I am supposed to be studying. Once a week.

    _____

13. **Can you make a PowerPoint presentation?** *Prezi? Do you like group projects?*
    I don't know PowerPoint yet, but I have three presentations this semester, so I'm going to learn ASAP.

    _____

14. **How often do you check your email?** *How often do you go to Facebook?*
    What's email? Just kidding. I don't use email much anymore. I usually send text messages instead.

    _____

15. **Do you have a good camera?** *Do you take a lot of photos or an average amount?*
    I have a big Canon SLR digital camera. It's big to carry around, but the pictures are awesome.

    _____

16. **What will your next tech purchase be?** *Where will you go shopping?*
    I need instant gratification, so I want a new iPad now! But I have to save up the money first.

    _____

Write your own question: _____

| Really? | No kidding? | No way! | Me too! | Bummer. | Anyway. |
| It depends. | For example? | Where? | When? | Why? | Who? | How? | How often? |

What about you?

MODEL CONVERSATION

At home, listen and repeat five times. Your pronunciation will DEFINITELY improve.

Brad	Hey, Britney, what's new?
Britney	I saw you yesterday, Brad.
Brad	Fine. Ask me what's new with me.
Britney	OK. What's new with you, Brad?
Brad	Check out my new iPhone! I got it yesterday after school. It's brand-new.
Britney	Wow. You mentioned something yesterday morning, but I didn't think you would buy one so quickly.
Brad	Oh, no. I'm an <u>instant gratification</u> kind of guy. I want it, and I want it now.
Britney	Lucky you. What kind of data plan did you get?
Brad	What's a data plan? Focus! Check this out: Call Britney.
Britney	Well . . .
Brad	Oops. I think it called my Aunt Britney in America. I hope I don't get charged.
Britney	OK, easy question. How many <u>gigabytes</u>?
Brad	Oh, I know, I know. Sixty-four. Well, I know how many I have, but I'm still not sure what they are.
Britney	That's what I figured. Where did you get it?
Brad	I got it in Myeong-dong. The camera is awesome. I think it is 10 or 12 megapixels. Whatever that is.
Britney	Have you taken any videos yet?
Brad	Yeah, I posted some on my Facebook page this morning.
Britney	Cool. Did you get any <u>accessories</u>?
Brad	Like what?
Britney	One of those snazzy holders that also carries your cash and credit cards and memory stick.
Brad	Oh heck. I forgot.
Britney	Did you get an arm strap for when you go jogging?
Brad	You think I am ever going to sweat on this baby? No way.
Britney	Sorry. Hey, let's take a <u>selfie</u>.
Brad	OK, watch this. iPhone, take a photo! [click]
Britney	Neat. But I think you can just say "photo." [click]
Brad	Hey, you were right!

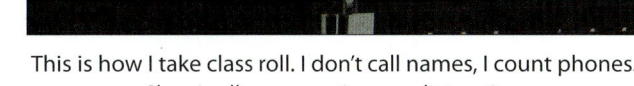

This is how I take class roll. I don't call names, I count phones. Class is all conversation, no distraction.

My Top 3 Electronics Wish List
1
2
3

TOP 4 CULTURAL DIFFERENCES

These cultural differences can also be conversation starters. You can ask:
What do you think about number 1? How do you feel about number 2? Which way do you prefer?

1. In Korea, when a phone takes a picture it must make a sound. That is the law. Not so in America.
2. It is common in Korea to buy groceries online and have them delivered. This is less common in America.
3. Korean Internet speeds are much faster than those in America.
4. Korean teenagers and college kids send and get hundreds of text messages a day. Americans typically do not send as many.

CULTURE QUESTIONS
What do you think of cell phone tracking? Would you care if your mother tracked you?
Do you agree with the law that requires phones to make a noise when a photo is taken?
What are the pros and cons of social networking sites?

Multi-tasking. Almost.

VOCABULARY DEVELOPMENT

ACROSS
1. This _____ must be wrong. We can't be there.
5. Will you get the disc or _____ the program?
7. If your computer freezes, you should _____ and see if that helps.
8. _____ messages are so annoying.
11. Click on that _____ that looks like an microphone.
13. How big is your _____? Twenty-one inches?

DOWN
1. I want it NOW. I need instant _____.
2. She can't be that skinny. They used _____.
3. You think that's a real iPhone for $20? You're too _____.
4. Heck, it _____ again. Time for a new computer.
6. Look at this _____ I took at the health club. Check out those killer abs!
9. I hate _____ messages. I would rather talk.
10. You ought to _____ around for a better price.
12. Did you remember to _____ out?

38

LONGER & SMOOTHER SPEAKING

Write about your three most important tech gadgets.

You can write about three devices or one device and three reasons. It's your life, so write about what you want.

My favorite device is my 27-inch iMac. I just love the big screen. I also have an external <u>monitor</u>, so I can write my essays on the iMac monitor and search for information on the Internet with the other monitor. This saves me a lot of time. And the Mac has a whole terabyte of <u>memory</u>, which is plenty to store all my videos. Also, I've started getting audio iBooks. I read them on the big screen and listen at the same time.

Second is my iPhone. Frankly, I don't use my phone much as a phone. I don't call people that much and I certainly do not want to waste my time typing on a phone. In class, I set up my phone to record, and then when I get home, I can replay the professor's lecture. And sometimes I listen to lectures on my subway ride home. I also like taking photos and videos. The photos are good, and the videos are awesome.

Third, I like my iPad. I like reading, and I have a long subway ride every day to and from school, so I read. The iPad is small enough to be portable and big enough so that it is not tiring on the eyes. And it's big enough that I can easily type emails and text messages. Phones are just too small for that. And the great thing is that all three devices easily talk to each other.

You could type it on computer and tape it above. This would check your spelling and grammar! Cool.

CONVERSATION

**Ask any question and start a conversation. Ask any group of questions. Or use the die.
If a conversation starts, go with it. Conversation is KING.**

Try to use new vocabulary. The more vocabulary you use on the conversation test, the higher your grade will be.

How many text messages do you send per day?
How many do you get?
About how much time do you spend texting per day?

What programs are you an expert in?
How did you learn?
Did you take a course?
Go to an academy?

What is your favorite computer game?
What is the longest you have ever played?
How often do you play?
Where do you play?

Do you belong to social networking sites?
Do you have a whole bunch of friends?
How much time do you spend per week on these sites?

Do you know any art programs, like Flash, Photoshop, Illustrator?
How did you learn them?
What do you use them for?

Have you ever downloaded anything illegally?
Do you download movies?
Music?
How often do you do that?
Shame!

Is email an important part of your life?
How often do you check your email?
Check it on your computer?

Do you follow a celebrity online?
In person? (Joke.)
Who? How often?
Since when?

Do you ever tweet? In English? What about?
Do you follow any English speakers?

LIKE to DISLIKE

1	love	I love my new iPhone. It's awesome.
2	really like	I really like watching YouTube.
3	enjoy	I enjoy reading on my iPad Mini.
4	so-so	My wrist phone is so-so.
5	don't mind	I don't mind using Excel.
6	don't care for	I don't care for the photo quality.
7	don't like	I don't like the button placement.
8	hate	I hate taking selfies. I look goofy.

FAVORITES

1.	My favorite	is the iPad Mini.
2	I like . . . the most	Canon cameras.
3	I like . . . more than	Sony . . . Panasonic.
4	I prefer	video games to reading.
5	If I had my choice,	I'd never use email again.
6	I'd rather not	use voice recognition.
7	If I could, I would	play video games all day.
8	My least favorite	news site is CNN.

Really? No way! Me too! Say what? Bummer.
Kind of. Half and half. It depends. Sometimes. For example?
Where? How often? How many? How big? What size? How much?

STATION

> But hey, first, what about some current events?
> What did you do last night?   Last weekend?   Last summer vacation?
> What will you do after class?   Tonight?   This weekend?   This winter vacation?

 4   **5**   **6**

Do you ever read blogs?
Which search engine do you use?
Do you get your news from TV or the Internet?

Do you have an expensive camera?
What kind? How much?
Do you have it with you?
Where did you get it?

How many selfies have you taken with your phone?
How many regular photos?

Do you ever video chat?
With someone overseas?
For how long?
Do you clean your room first?

How many phones have you had in your life?
Do you get hand-me-down phones from your parents?
Who pays for your phones?

Have you ever posted a video online?
What site did you put it on?
Tell me about it.
Can you give me the address?

Do you have a printer in your bedroom?
Do you ever use a computer at school?

How many phones have you lost?
Was alcohol involved?
How many have you found?

Do you have any Apple products?
Have you ever used a Mac computer?

AGREE & DISAGREE

It's more expensive, but it's the best value.

1 If you say so.   Are you sure?
2 Me too.   I doubt it.
3 I agree.   I disagree.
4 I think so too.   I don't think so.
5 I feel the same way.   Impossible.
6 I hear that.   No way.
7 Absolutely.   In your dreams.

COMPARISON

IT WAS TOO	THIS ONE IS MORE / LESS
1 complicated	affordable
2 expensive / cheap	comfortable
3 heavy / light	convenient
4 high-tech / old-fashioned	expensive
5 thick / thin / tight / baggy	user-friendly
6 wide / narrow	quiet / noisy
7 small / big	HAS more / less memory

What about you?

4 DATING & NIGHTLIFE

Scan and find the tracks.

Psst. Guys, funny is good.

 22

Vocabulary Vitamins

admired from afar	선망의 대상인	Out of sight, out of mind.	눈에서 멀어지면 마음도 멀어진다
baggage	사적인 문제	out of your league	신분에 맞지 않는
blind date	소개팅	picky	까다로운
break up	이별하다, 헤어지다	play Cupid	데이트를 주선하다
cheap date	돈을 잘 쓰지 않는 데이트 상대	play hard to get	튕기는
cheap drunk	술에 자주 취하는 사람	puppy love	어릴 적 첫사랑
cheat on	바람 피우다	secret admirer	누군가 나 모르게 좋아하는 사람
chemistry	이성 간의 끌림	soul mate	잘 통하는 짝
have a crush on	사랑에 빠진, 반하다	stand up	바람을 맞히다
dating around	여러 명과 만나는	tease	약올리다
going steady	꾸준히 사귀고 있는	the silent treatment	침묵시위
Dear John letter	이별의 편지	two-timer	바람난 사람
fix up	데이트를 주선하다	unrequited love	짝사랑
flirt	장난 삼아 연애하다	whirlwind romance	아주 빠르게 진행된 사랑
going steady	한 사람만 사귀는		
hit on	수작 걸다	**EXACT RELATIONSHIP**	
long-distance romance	멀리 떨어져서 사랑하는 사람들	platonic friend	우애적인 이성 친구
love at first sight	첫 눈에 반한 사랑	boyfriend / girlfriend	남자친구 / 여자친구 (사귀는 사이)
love is blind	사랑에 눈이 멀다	steady boyfriend / girlfriend	오랫동안 사귄 애인
love triangle	삼각관계	lover	섹스 파트너; 애인
lust / love	욕정 / 사랑	**DRINKING**	
make up with	다시 잘 해보다	black out; pass out	정신을 잃다
mama's boy	엄마에게 심하게 의존하는 남자	buzzed; tipsy; drunk	기분 좋게 취하다; 여자들이 살짝 취하다; 취하다
Mr. Right / Miss Right	본인에게 완벽한 남자 / 여자	hangover, hungover	숙취
opposites attract	극끼리 통한다	slurring his/her words	혀가 꼬이다

What are the two worst sentences in the English language? 1. *We've got to talk.* 2. *But we can still be friends.*

42

 23 **CONVERSATION STARTERS**

You'll need to interview your parents for this unit. Take notes.
EXTRA POINTS if you bring some of their dating photos.

1. **How did your parents meet?** *How long did they date? What is their age gap?*
   My parents met at college. They were a campus couple. They dated for four years and broke up twice.

2. **Do you believe in love at first sight?** *How many times has it happened to you?*
   I definitely believe in love at first sight. The problem is that most times it is only one-sided.

3. **Did your mother's parents like your father at first?** *What about your father's parents?*
   My father is a doctor, so my mother's parents liked him from the start.

4. **Did your mother play hard to get?** *Have you ever played hard to get?*
   My mother says she did not play hard to get, but my father says she did. I hope to get details soon.

5. **Have you ever had a crush on someone?** *Have you ever admired someone from afar?*
   I had a crush on this jock in high school. He was out of my league, but he was so cute.

6. **What advice did your parents give you about boys/girls?** *Do you follow it?*
   My mother told me never to hang around boys who are drinking heavily.

7. **How long did your parents date before your mom knew he was "the one"?**
   Mom says she knew he was the one right away, but she was worried about marrying the oldest son.

8. **What is your best quality that will help you get a boy/girlfriend?**
   Well, I am a nice, sincere, honest person. But if I were taller, I think that might help a lot.

Really?   No kidding.   No way!   Me too!   Bummer.   Anyway.
It depends.   For example?   Where?   When?   Why?   Who?   How?   How often?

What about you?

CONVERSATION STARTERS

9. **Do you have a boyfriend/girlfriend?** *Are you a campus couple? Same major? This class?*
   Well, I had a girlfriend until last weekend. We were a campus couple, and she's sitting over there!

   _____

10. **Which is your big night, Friday or Saturday?** *What do you usually do?*
    Both. I party with school friends near campus on Friday and in Hongdae on Saturday.

    _____

11. **What is your favorite drink?** *Have you ever drunk so much you can't remember?*
    I drink anything, and all beers taste the same to me. I like dongdongju *and* haemul pajeon.

    _____

12. **Can you have fun without drinking?** *Have you ever had to carry a friend who passed out?*
    Once, I didn't drink because I was taking some medicine, and frankly, it was boring. So I prefer drinking.

    _____

13. **Have you ever gotten home after sunrise?** *What is the latest you ever got home?*
    I've never gotten home after sunrise, because I told my mom I was sleeping at a friend's house.

    _____

14. **Have you ever had a blind date?** **(NOT** *meeting***)** *How many times? Have you ever been stood up?*
    I had a group blind date. Four boys and four girls. It was OK. The girls were pretty but not interested in us.

    _____

15. **Have you ever said no to someone who asked you for a date?**
    Yes, I was in a beer bar near school and this girl hit on me, but I was too surprised and said no.

    _____

16. **If your boyfriend/girlfriend looked just like a movie star, which one would it be?**
    Hyun Bin. He has a great smile. Or Won Bin. He looks intense. / Lee Hyo-ri or Nam Gyu-ri.

    _____

Write your own question: _____

> Really?   No kidding.   No way!   Me too!   Bummer.   Anyway.
> It depends.   For example?   Where?   When?   Why?   Who?   How?   How often?

What about you?

MODEL CONVERSATION

Brad   Hey, Britney, who was that good-looking guy that I saw you with at the library?

Britney   Oh, that was Bob Taylor.

Brad   Is he your boyfriend?

Britney   No, he's just a friend. I've known him since elementary school.

Brad   Come on, you two looked pretty chummy. I thought I saw sparks.

Britney   No, really. His girlfriend is studying in America, and I just keep him company. Free meals for me, and he doesn't get bored sitting at home all the time. Say, how was your <u>blind date</u> last weekend?

Brad   She had a <u>nice personality</u>.

Britney   Ouch. OK, besides not being beautiful, what was wrong with her?

Brad   Aw, she was OK, I guess. She just wasn't my type.

Britney   What is your type? You're just too <u>picky</u>!

Brad   I'm not picky. I just have high standards. I'm saving myself for <u>Miss Right</u>.

Britney   Yeah, right. Tell me about it. You're not going to meet <u>Miss Right</u> in a bar, you know.

Brad   It's possible. Besides, I'm too shy to talk to women without alcohol.

Britney   No, you're just too <u>superficial</u>. You're only concerned with their looks. If they don't look like a cheerleader, you're not interested.

Brad   Say what? No. I'm a lonely, sensitive, caring guy.

Britney   Lonely? You're out with a different girl every night of the week.

Brad   There, you see? That means that I'm lonely but looking very hard.

Britney   Yeah, right. And I'm Hyolyn.

Brad   And what about you? You're <u>picky</u> also. You only had two dates with Jake, and then you wouldn't see him anymore.

Britney   He turned out to be a <u>nerd</u>.

Brad   Yeah, but a rich nerd.

Britney   That's why I went on the second date. It was my birthday. Do you really think I'm going to break up with a rich guy BEFORE my birthday?

Brade   Oh, that's <u>cold</u>, Britney.

Rank your top qualities 1 - 6

Body	
Face	
Height	
Intelligence	
Money	
Personality	

The qualities I hate most are

Heavy drinker	
Smoker	
Too poor	
Too short	
Unfaithful	
Violent	

ROMANTIC OPPOSITES

affectionate; touchy-feely	1	cold fish; cold
break up in person	2	change your phone number
faithful	3	playgirl/playboy
forgive and forget	4	hold a grudge
girl-next-door type	5	*femme fatale*
lead somebody on	6	be led on
low-maintenance	7	high-maintenance
trusting	8	jealous; possessive
material girl	9	spiritual girl

DRINKING OPPOSITES

매우 인기 있는 여자	belle of the ball	wallflower	파트너가 없는 여자
폭음하는 사람	binge drinker	teetotaler	술을 절대 마시지 않는 사람
아침에 매우 일찍 일어나는 사람	early bird	night owl	새벽에 활동적인 사람
즐겁게 술을 마시는 사람	happy drunk	unhappy drunk	술을 마시면 침울해지는 사람 / 못되게 구는 사람
알콜내성이 높아 술을 잘 마시는	high tolerance	low tolerance	알콜내성이 낮아 술을 잘 못마시는
파티 분위기를 살리는 사람	life of the party	wet blanket	흥을 깨는 사람
파티를 매우 좋아하는 파티광	party animal	party pooper	파티의 흥을 깨는 사람
주말에 집중적으로 술마시는 사람	weekend warrior	social drinker	사교를 위해 술을 마시는 사람

TOP 5 CULTURAL DIFFERENCES

These cultural differences can also be conversation starters. You can ask:
What do you think about number 1? How do you feel about number 2? Which way do you prefer?

1. If a Korean's parents do not like their son or daughter's choice of husband or wife, they can forbid the marriage. This is definitely not the American way.
2. Korea has Valentine's Day and White Day (and a Black Day). America has only Valentine's Day, and on this day, men do most of the giving.
3. Americans introduce their boyfriends and girlfriends to their parents much sooner, and it carries no special significance. When Koreans introduce their boyfriend or girlfriend to their parents, it means that the relationship is serious.
4. In Korea, the custom is for friends to pour your drinks for you. There's nothing like that in America.
5. "Campus couple" is a great descriptive term, but there is no such term in America.

My parents while dating. They are both *pretending* to be social drinkers. Actually, my mother was a teetotaler, and my father was a weekend warrior.

CULTURE QUESTIONS
Is there too much social stigma on divorce and remarriage in Korea?
Should parents have power over whom their children marry?
Are there too many romantic holidays that put emphasis on having a boyfriend or girlfriend?

VOCABULARY DEVELOPMENT

ACROSS
3. I'll date _____ for a while before going steady.
5. You're too _____. Nobody is good enough for you.
7. I was too shy. I only admired her from _____.
8. I was _____ when she turned me down.
9. Do you want a _____ date with my cousin?
11. Oh, he's the one. He's my _____ mate.
13. We've been going _____ for almost a year.
14. She's a _____. She likes attention; she doesn't like you.
15. She's giving me the _____ treatment. Bummer.

DOWN
1. Oh no. He has too much _____. No way.
2. That's just _____ love. You'll get over it.
4. She's Miss Korea! Way out of your _____.
6. I tried to play _____, but they both said no.
8. In high school, I had a _____ on the class leader. Oh, so cute.
9. Bummer. When did you _____ up?
10. He's gone abroad. Out of _____, out of mind.
11. He's a nice guy. Don't _____ him on just to see his homework.

LONGER & SMOOTHER SPEAKING

Write about your ideal mate.
Or write about how your parents met. Or both.

My Mr. Right will be tall and good-looking, but not too good-looking. I do not like people who are <u>vain</u>. And if my boyfriend is really handsome, too many girls will <u>flirt</u> with him. A very good-looking mate can be <u>high-maintenance</u>. I'd like somebody who is affectionate, but not affectionate in public. But I don't want a <u>cold fish</u>, either. Of course, my ideal man must be <u>faithful</u>. And he must trust me. I don't like <u>jealous</u> or <u>possessive</u> boyfriends. I believe in <u>love at first sight</u> because my father says that's what happened to him. He saw my mom in a restaurant near work and thought, "I'm going to marry her." Mom says that story is not true, but Dad swears it is. But they did have a <u>whirlwind romance</u>. They dated for only six months before getting married. Mom said she tried to <u>play hard to get</u>, but Dad was just too cute. Her mom told her when she was a teenager: Find guys who make you laugh and marry the best-looking one.

Funny story: Mom says that one of the things she liked about Dad was that he was not a heavy drinker. Actually, Dad was a <u>weekend warrior</u>. He was just smart enough never to drink heavily around her. Some people told her that he drank, but she did not believe them until their honeymoon. She said after she found out, she gave him the <u>silent treatment</u> for two hours, but then, like she always says, he's just too cute.

You could type it on computer and tape it above. This would check your spelling and grammar! Cool.

CONVERSATION

Open your book. Your partner closes their book.
Turn the book sideways to that you can see this page, and your partner can see the other page.
Nobody can see their partner's questions.

1. Are you more likely to be the belle of the ball or a wallflower?
Are you a good dancer?

Do you forgive and forget or hold a grudge?
Is there anyone you are peeved at (angry) now? Why?
It's not me, is it?

Have you ever led somebody on? (Just a little?)
Has somebody ever led you on?
Somebody in this class?

Is your girlfriend a material girl?
Are you going into debt dating her?
Did you meet her at church?
Did you buy her a Gucci bag?

3. Would you break up in person or send a text message?
How would you prefer to get the news?

Was your mother the girl-next-door type or a *femme fatale*?
Did she date a lot before finding your father?

Are you spontaneous, or do you need advance notice?
What is the last spontaneous thing you did?

Girls: How often do you pay for the evening?
Guys: How often does your girlfriend pay?

5. Have you ever stood somebody up?
Why did you agree in the first place? (Too much alcohol?)
Have you ever broken a date?

Is your father an affectionate, touchy-feely kind of guy or a cold fish?
Is he romantic?
Does he cry at movies?

Is your girlfriend high-maintenance?
What did you buy her for 100 days? For her birthday? Pepperro?

Are you the trusting type or the jealous type?
How trusting?
What if their project partner is VERY attractive?

Really? No kidding. Say what? Me too Bummer.
Where? When? Why? Who? How? How long? How often?
Kind of. Sometimes. Half and half. It depends.

What about you?

STATION

Ask any question and start a conversation. Ask any group of questions.
Or use the die. It it lands with 3 up, ask a 3 question. Talk about all the 3 questions, or roll again.
This is not interview class. It's conversation class. When a conversation starts, *go go go*.

6

Have you ever been stood up?
How long did you wait before you gave up?
Did you feel dumb for waiting so long?

Would you marry a rich mama's boy?
Would you marry the oldest son?
Would you marry a divorced person?

Girls, would you date anyone younger than you?
Shorter than you?
Are you dating them now?

How many blind dates have you been on?
Have you ever played cupid?
(Arrange a blind date for a friend)
How did it turn out?

What about you?

4

Have you ever had a crush on a platonic friend who didn't feel the same way?
You poor thing.

Can you hold your liquor?
(Can you drink a lot?)
What's your favorite drink?
Beer? Soju? Makgeoli?
Baek seju? Dongdongju?

Would you ever date a foreigner?
What would your father think if you did?
Would you ever date a foreigner and lie to your parents about it?

Have you ever gotten the silent treatment?
How long did it last?
How many times did you apologize?

Say what?   Me too.   Bummer.
How?   How long?   How often?
Half and half.   It depends.

2

Are you a weekend warrior or a social drinker?
How much did you drink last weekend?
Last night?

How did your parents meet?
Was it love at first sight?
Do you believe in love at first sight?

Do your parents like your boyfriend/girlfriend?
Did they meet by accident?
How many times have they met?

Have you ever admired someone from afar?
Ever had a crush on someone?
Ever been crushed (heartbroken)?
Are you crushed now? Bummer.

Really?   No kidding.   No way!
Where?   When?   Why?   Who?
Kind of.   Sometimes.

5 Sofa Time
TV, Music, & Reading

Scan and find the tracks.

What did you do last Sunday afternoon?

Noon

1:00

2:00

3:00 - 6:00

Oh, I cleaned my room, studied, and prepared for my classes.

 27

Vocabulary Vitamins

TV TERMS	TV SHOWS		MOVIE GENRES	MOVIE TERMS
bloopers	animation	infomercial	action-adventure	character actor
channel surfer	awards show	melodrama	animation	chemistry
commercial	cartoon	music; music variety	comedy	dialog-driven
freeze frame	celebrity game show	nature	historical drama	ensemble cast
laugh track	children's education	news	horror	far-fetched
lip-sync	comedy	political	musical	*femme fatale*
prime time (NOT golden)	concert	reality TV	prison film	flashback
repeat; rerun	cooking	religious	romance	girl-next-door type
slow motion	costume drama	home shopping	science fiction	macho
theme song	docudrama	sitcom (situation comedy)	**BASIC PLOTS**	plot twist
TV PEOPLE	documentary	soap opera	boy meets girl	predictable
anchorman / woman	drama	sports	amnesia	remake
announcer	education	talk show	buddy film	sequel
celebrity	financial	trash TV	Cinderella story	sidekick
director / producer	fitness; exercise	travel	coming-of-age	snooty rich type
host; co-host; MC	health	variety	love triangle	villain

50

CONVERSATION STARTERS

1. **What is your favorite TV program?** *Who are the stars? When does it come on?*
   My favorite show is no longer on. It was My Love from Space *with Jeon Ji-hyun and Kim Su-hyun.*

2. **How many hours do you watch TV every day?** *On Saturday? On Sunday?*
   I watch TV about two hours every weekday. Four hours on Saturday and about six on Sunday. I like TV.

3. **What kind of music do you like?** *What kind of music do you hate?*
   I like dance music. It gives me energy. My favorite song is "Candy" by Baek Ji-hyun. I HATE rap music.

4. **Who's your favorite Korean male singer or group?** *Female singer or group?*
   I think most of the male singers are Rain wannabes—all the same. I like Hyolyn in Sistar.

5. **Can you sing?** *Do you play a musical instrument? Is your family musically inclined?*
   Well, I think I can sing, but nobody agrees. My family is musically inclined. We all play an instrument.

6. **What kind of TV shows do your parents watch?** *Do they stay up late watching TV?*
   My father watches the news and sports, and my mom likes the evening soap operas.

7. **Do you like to read?** *What kind of books or magazines? Do you read books in English?*
   I like to read. I mainly read history and biographies of famous people, like Napoleon or Caesar.

8. **Do you get your news from TV, newspapers, or the Internet?** *Do you prefer KBS? SBS?*
   I get my news mainly from TV, and I'll go to the Internet for background information. I like the Chosun Ilbo.

Really?	No kidding.	No way!	Me too!	Bummer.	Anyway.
Kind of.	Half and half.	Sometimes.	It depends.	For example?	
Where?	When?	Why?	Who?	How?	What time?	How often?

What about you?

 29

CONVERSATION STARTERS

9. **Have you ever seen a TV or movie or singing star in person?** *Were they tall?*
   I saw Lady Gaga when she came to Seoul. She was shorter than I thought.
   _____

10. **Who is your favorite TV actor? Actress?** *Who is your favorite TV comedian?*
    My favorite actor and actress are Hyun Bin and Song Hye-kyo. I like Yoo Jae-suk. I hear he's a nice guy.
    _____

11. **What is your favorite Korean movie?** *Your favorite American movie?*
    My favorite Korean movie is Roaring Currents. Guardians of the Galaxy *is my favorite American film.*
    _____

12. **What is your favorite movie genre?** *What kind of movies do you hate?*
    I like historical dramas and romantic comedies, and I hate horror movies and gory slasher movies.
    _____

13. **Would you prefer to watch reruns or surf the Internet?** *Why?*
    If those were my only two choices, I would read a book. I have lots of books on my iPad.
    _____

14. **Can you study with the TV on?** *With the radio on? Do you have a long attention span?*
    I need absolute quiet when I study. When I was younger, I could listen to music, but not anymore.
    _____

15. **Have you ever been to a pop music concert?** *Did they lip-sync?*
    I went to a girl-group concert in Jamsil last year. They all lip-synced. I saw Psy once. He sang live.
    _____

16. **Do you legally download movies or music?** *How many songs do you own?*
    My father is a government official, so I never do anything illegal! I have about two thousand songs.
    _____

Write your own question: _____

| Really? | No kidding. | No way! | Me too! | Bummer. | Anyway. |
| It depends. | For example? | Where? | When? | Why? | Who? | How? | How often? |

What about you?

 30

MODEL CONVERSATION

At home, listen and repeat five times. Your pronunciation will DEFINITELY improve.

Britney	Hi. Before we start talking about today's topic, what did you do last night?
Brad	Let's see. I watched TV. What about you?
Britney	I went to the library and prepared for this class. Well, what did you do last weekend?
Brad	I watched TV.
Britney	Really? Are you a professional <u>couch potato</u>? Is that all you do?
Brad	No, silly. I was preparing for this class. The topic is Sofa Time! TV time! I even <u>pulled an all-nighter</u>.
Britney	Finally, a topic you're interested in.
Brad	Absolutely. I'm a TV expert. I grew up on TV.
Britney	OK, let's have it. What did you watch?
Brad	Oh, I saw a new genre of TV show. It's a musical <u>soap opera</u>.
Britney	Really? Good research. Tell me more.
Brad	Yeah, it's based on a movie sequel. Remember the movie Mamma Mia?
Britney	Sure. But I didn't know they made a sequel to Mamma Mia.
Brad	They did. It was called Grandmamma Mia.
Britney	Get a life.
Brad	What kind of shows do you like?
Britney	I like the <u>top-40</u> live music programs. I like the dancing and <u>choreography</u>.
Brad	I like them too, but I wish they would sing live instead of <u>lip-syncing</u>.
Britney	True. And after one group has a hit song, there are a bunch of <u>wannabe</u> groups imitating them.
Brad	Yeah, that happens a lot with the <u>boy bands</u>. <u>Girl groups</u> too.
Britney	What kind of shows do your parents watch?
Brad	My mom likes <u>melodramas</u>.
Britney	My mom too, but my father hates them. He likes history <u>documentaries</u>.
Brad	Does your father read a lot?
Britney	A lot. He doesn't like <u>fiction</u>. He mainly reads history—a lot of <u>biographies</u>.
Brad	My mother reads a lot, but only <u>romantic mysteries</u>.
Britney	Really? For example?
Brad	Well, I don't remember the titles, but she's always asking my father, "Tell me again—why did I marry you?"

BOOKS
animation
biography
comic book
fiction
non-fiction
humor
mystery
romance
self-help
travel

MAGAZINES
fashion
fitness
health
movie
sports
travel

MUSIC TYPES
ballad
classical
country
dance
disco
gospel; religious
hard rock
heavy metal
jazz
R & B
rap
rock and roll
techno pop
top 40

MUSIC TERMS
boy band
choreography
concert
download
file sharing
girl group
light show
lip-sync
MP3
one-hit wonder
pirate
soundtrack
streaming
wannabe

TOP 5 CULTURAL DIFFERENCES

These cultural differences can also be conversation starters. You can ask:
What do you think about number 1? How do you feel about number 2? Which way do you prefer?

1. Most American prime-time TV shows come on only once a week. When they are in reruns, they might come on Monday through Friday.
2. The average American TV series lasts a lot longer than the average Korean one. Some popular American shows, such as *CSI*, last for more than ten years.
3. America has 24-hour news, sports, and financial channels.
4. American TV commercials can come on at any time, whereas Korean TV commercials are usually grouped all together at the beginning and end of a program.
5. American TV is more violent and shows more sexual content than Korean TV.

MY FAVORITES
Male Korean TV star
Female Korean TV star
M American movie star
F American movie star
Korean comedian
Korean TV show
Book
Singer or group

CULTURE QUESTIONS

Korean TV blurs out cigarettes and knives. Is this helping save Korea's youth?
Compare Korean and American singers and music shows.
Who are the most creative people in the Korean entertainment industry?
Are there any dangers to reality TV? Do you think audition programs build unrealistic hopes?

VOCABULARY DEVELOPMENT

ACROSS
6. The _____ were funnier than the actual show.
7. Sylvestor Stallone always plays the _____ man.
9. My brother is a channel _____. He has a short attention span.
11. Aw, the same old plot. Another love _____.
12. Whoa. That scene was too sexy for _____ time.

DOWN
1. Spider-Man always fights a different _____.
2. Brad and Angelina have great screen _____.
3. The was the biggest _____ cast I've ever seen.
4. The movie was all _____-driven. No action.
5. Bummer, nothing on tonight but _____ operas.
8. If the movie's a hit, they always make a _____.
9. She plays the same perky character in every _____. Do something different. Act!
10. They made a _____ of *My Sassy Girl* in America.

54

LONGER & SMOOTHER SPEAKING

Write about your favorite TV show, singer or group, and book.
Or write about your three favorite TV shows or singers or books.

My favorite TV show is The Big Bang Theory. *It's an American sitcom about three science nerds in Los Angeles and their relationships with women. The show has several <u>stereotypes</u>: the dumb blond waitress trying to be an actress, the nerd who has a domineering mother, and a super-nerd who is so smart he has trouble understanding normal human emotions. There is also an Indian guy with a thick accent who is often puzzled by American culture.*

My favorite singing group is Maroon 5. Their voices are just so harmonious. I saw them when they came to Seoul a few years ago. I really like the fact that they are talented enough to sing live. They don't lip-sync. They all have great voices, and they sing with such sincerity.

Also, I like to read a lot. I have over a hundred books, mainly history and <u>biography</u>. I never read <u>fiction</u>. Lately, I've been reading a lot on the Internet. After watching a movie or TV show, I'll go to the Internet and read all about it and the actors. My next project is to get audio books and read them and listen at the same time. I want to find books that have good vocabulary that I can learn.

You could type it on computer and tape it above. This would check your spelling and grammar! Cool.

CONVERSATION

Ask any question and start a conversation. Ask any group of questions. Or use the die.

1 DESCRIBING

Describe your favorite Korean movie, **but don't tell me the name** so I can try to guess.
Why do you like it?
How many times have you seen it?
What is your favorite scene?

Describe your favorite Korean movie star, their appearance and movies, **but don't tell me their name** so I can try to guess.

Describe your favorite singer or group. **Don't tell me their name** so I can try to guess. How many members? What kind of music?

Describe your favorite American movie, **but don't tell me the name** so I can try to guess.
Why do you like it?
How many times have you seen it?
What is your favorite scene?

Describe your favorite American movie star, their appearance and movies. **Don't tell me their name** so I can try to guess.

2 FAVORITES

Where do you get your news? Newspaper, Internet, TV?

What is your favorite TV channel? KBS, SBS, MBC, Fox?

What kind of music do you hate? Which singer or group?

What kind of movies do you hate?

What is your favorite TV show? Why do you like it?

What is your favorite book? Are you a fast reader?

What is your favorite TV commercial? Which commercial do you hate?

3 COMPARISON

Do you prefer musicals or animated movies? Comedies or dramas?

Which do you like more, romantic movies or horror movies?

Do you like classic movies or modern movies? Color or black & white?

Do you prefer Korean or foreign movies?

Which do you like more, Japanese or Chinese movies?

Do you prefer ballads, dance music, or rap music?

Do you prefer shopping on the Internet or in stores?

MOVIE GUESSING QUESTIONS: When does it take place? Where does it take place? How long a time span does it cover? Is it a classic or modern movie? Does it have a sequel? Is it a true story? Does it have an ensemble cast? How old are the stars? Is the director famous? Did it win any Academy Awards? What is the basic plot? Do any of the stars look like me?

STATION

If a conversation starts, go with it. Conversation is KING.
Try to use new vocabulary. The more vocabulary you use on the conversation test, the higher your grade will be.

4 DURATION	5 FREQUENCY	6 WHATEVER
What is the last movie that you saw? How long ago? Where? Who?	How often does your whole family watch a movie together?	What kind of movies do your parents like? Do they watch a lot of TV?
Do you play a musical instrument? How long have you played?	What is your parents' favorite TV show? How often does it come on?	How many MP3s do you have? Where do you download them from?
Have you ever seen a movie star or celebrity in person? When? Where?	Do you ever cry at movies? Which movie did you cry at the most?	Do you ever go to the movies with your parents? Ever go alone?
How many hours do you watch TV on Sunday? What do you watch?	How often do you download movies? Legally?	Who is your favorite TV comedian or MC? Ever seen them in person?
What is the longest you ever surfed the Internet?	How often do you watch TV for six hours straight?	Who is your favorite female TV celebrity? Is she also a model?
How many hours do you watch TV during the week?	How often do you watch English movies? Without subtitles?	What is the worst movie you have ever seen?
How many hours do you watch TV on Saturday? What do you watch?	How often do you play a computer game? For five hours straight?	What is your favorite movie series? (*Iron Man, Spider-Man*?)

What about you?

Really? You're kidding. No kidding. No way. Say what? Bummer. Me too.
Where? When? Why? Who? What time? How? How long? How often?
Kind of. Sort of. Sometimes. Half and half. It depends. For example?

6 Health & Fitness

Scan and find the tracks.

They say that Yoga is good for both mental and physical health. They say.

Plan B.

 32

Vocabulary Vitamins

ache	통증	itch	간지러움
addicted, addiction	중독	nauseous	구역질나는
allergic, allergy	알레르기의, 알레르기	pain: dull / sharp	통증, 둔통 / 만성적 통증
allergic reaction	알레르기 반응	paralyzed	마비된
blister	물집	pimple; zit / acne	뾰루지 / 여드름
blood, bleeding	피 흘리는	pollen	꽃가루
blood type	혈액형: A,B,O,AB	prescription drugs	처방약
boil	종기, 부스럼	pulled muscle	접질린, 무리가 간 근육
bruised; black and blue	멍든	rash	발진
burned	화상입은	rehab, rehabilitation	물리치료
cancer	암	runs in the family / genes	가족력이 있는 / 혈통
cast / crutches	깁스 / 목발	scar	흉터
checkup	오한	seasick	멀미
clinic	클리닉	shot; injection	주사 (예방주사 등)
cold / flu / pneumonia	감기 / 독감 / 폐렴	sinuses	비강
cold turkey	나쁜 습관을 완전히 끊다	sore	쑤시는
CPR	심폐소생술	sore throat	목통증
diarrhea	설사	sprain	삠, 접질림
dizzy	현기증이 나는	stitches	꿰매기
drugstore / pharmacist	약국 / 약제사	stomach cramps	위경련
emergency room (ER)	응급실	stomachache	복통
faint; pass out; black out	기절하다	swell, swelling	부풀다
fever	열	tendon / ligament	건 / 인대
donate blood	헌혈	throw up; vomit	토하다 (NOT overeat)
Intensive Care Unit (ICU)	중환자실	tonsils	편도선

EYES	contacts	콘택트렌즈	TEETH	braces	치아 교정기
	LASIK eye surgery	라식수술		cavity	충치

58

CONVERSATION STARTERS

🎧 33

1. **Have you ever missed school because you were sick?** *How long were you out?*
   I broke my leg while snowboarding in middle school, and I missed a week of school.

2. **Do you catch bad colds or average ones?** *Do you catch colds in a certain season?*
   Yes, my colds are usually pretty bad. I used to go to school and suffer, but now I just stay home.

3. **When was the last time you went to the doctor?** *Do any health problems run in your family?*
   I went to the dentist last month for a cavity. Sinus allergies run in my family. Dust and pollen affect us.

4. **When you are sick or hurt, do you suffer in silence or complain a lot?** *Your father?*
   I complain like crazy, but my father is the strong, silent type. He never complains. He's macho.

5. **Have you ever fainted or passed out?** *Have you ever been cut, burned, or had a broken bone?*
   I fainted once in middle school. The sight of blood made me pass out. I hit my head. Ouch.

6. **What do you think of plastic surgery?** *What kind would you like?*
   Plastic surgery is often the price stars have to pay to make it to the big time. Sad, but true.

7. **Have you ever had a medical emergency?** *Ever seen an accident or emergency?*
   Kind of. There was a gas leak in high school, and they evacuated the whole school.

8. **What is your blood type?** *Do you believe it affects your personality?*
   My blood type is A. I think there may be something to that belief, but not much.

Really?	No kidding.	No way!	Me too!	Bummer.	Anyway.
Kind of.	Half and half.	Sometimes	It depends.	For example?
Where?	When?	Why?	Who?	How?	What time?	How often?

What about you?

CONVERSATION STARTERS  34

9. **What is your favorite sport or exercise?** *Watching or doing? Are you in shape?*
   My parents are into physical fitness, and I kind of follow along. We go mountain climbing once a month.

10. **Are you taking any PE classes this semester?** *Did you like PE in high school?*
    I'm taking a taekwondo class this semester. I like it. The instructor is a fitness fanatic. She's in great shape.

11. **How often do you exercise till you sweat?** *How often do you pig out?*
    I hate to exercise and love to pig out. Can you tell? Luckily, skinny genes run in my family.

12. **Have you ever gone on a crash diet?** *After Chuseok or Lunar New Year? How long?*
    I had a blind date once, and I dieted before that. Never again. Love me as I am, or not at all.

13. **Can you ski or snowboard?** *Can you swim? What sport would you like to be good at?*
    I can snowboard and ski. I'd like to be a tennis champion.

14. **Have you ever eaten food that made you sick?** *Are you allergic to anything?*
    Once, I ate too much and got sick. Does that count? Actually, I'm allergic to shellfish.

15. **Do you wear contacts?** *Would you like to get LASIK surgery?*
    Yes, I wear contacts, and I hope to get LASIK surgery this winter. I have been looking around at prices.

16. **Does your father smoke?** *Do you smoke? Would you ever marry someone who smokes?*
    My father used to smoke, but he quit cold turkey when he turned 40. I'd never marry a smoker.

Write your own question: _____

| Really? | No kidding. | No way! | Me too! | Bummer. | Anyway. |
| It depends. | For example? | Where? | When? | Why? | Who? | How? | How often? |

What about you?

MODEL CONVERSATION

Brad	Do you feel OK? You don't look so good.
Britney	I feel terrible. I had a bad <u>cold</u> all weekend.
Brad	Why don't you stay home?
Britney	No can do. My mother's a fanatic about attendance.
Brad	My mom's the same way. I have to be half dead to miss school. Do bad colds <u>run in your family</u>?
Britney	Yeah. We don't catch colds often, but when we do, they're bad.
Brad	Bummer. Do you go to the doctor or stay home?
Britney	Oh, my father and brother want to go to the hospital. They moan and groan and think they're dying. My mother and I are the macho ones.
Brad	Funny. You, macho. I can't imagine.
Britney	Anyway. And after the cold season passes, we all have <u>allergies</u> from the <u>pollen</u> and dust.
Brad	I can't imagine that. My family is always healthy. We don't diet, we eat and drink whatever we want, and never gain weight and never catch colds. Good <u>genes</u>.
Britney	Lucky you. Well, what happened to you? Why is your arm <u>black and blue</u>?
Brad	Oh, I was rollerblading and tried something new.
Britney	And failed, obviously.
Brad	Yeah. But a friend of mine took a video with his phone. Maybe I'll be famous on the Internet soon.
Britney	Dream on. What happened, exactly? That looks like a pretty bad <u>bruise</u>.
Brad	Really. It's turned several colors already. And my elbow was <u>swollen</u> yesterday and last night, but the <u>swelling</u> went down this morning.
Britney	Weren't you wearing a helmet and elbow and knee pads?
Brad	Real men don't wear those.
Britney	Right. Why don't you sit down? There's an empty seat.
Brad	I fell on my behind also. It hurts when I sit.

Match the doctors on the left with their specialties on the right.

1	2	cardiologist	1. animals
2		dentist	2. the heart
3		dermatologist	3. children
4		internist	4. cosmetic surgery
5		neurologist	5. crooked teeth
6		obstetrician, gynecologist (OB-GYN)	6. eyes
7		ophthalmologist	7. diseases in adults
8		orthodontist	8. using images to find disease
9		pediatrician	9. brain, nerves, nervous system
10		plastic surgeon	10. skin
11		radiologist	11. teeth
12		veterinarian (vet)	12. women's reproductive health

TOP 6 CULTURAL DIFFERENCES

These cultural differences can also be conversation starters. You can ask:
What do you think about number 1? How do you feel about number 2? Which way do you prefer?

1. American hospital patients are restricted to the hospital. They cannot or should not leave. Around Korean hospitals, patients in hospital gowns can be seen outside.
2. At an American supermarket you can buy a wide range of over-the-counter medicines, but not in Korea.
3. Korea has national health insurance. America is beginning to.
4. Chinese herbal medicine and acupuncture are common in Korea but less common in America.
5. Many Americans do not know their blood type, and even if they do, they do not believe it is related to their personality.
6. In Korean cities, there is a small pharmacy on just about every block. In America, pharmacies are bigger (and not as common), and big stores such as Wal-Mart have their own pharmacy inside.

Great news!
You can go back to school.

CULTURE QUESTIONS
*Do you think plastic surgery is too common in Korea?
Is there too much emphasis on looks in Korean society?
Are you proud that Korea is a top medical tourism destination?
Do you believe blood type determines personality? Give an example.*

VOCABULARY DEVELOPMENT

ACROSS

2. That's not just a cold—you have the _____.
5. One day, my father just quit smoking cold _____.
7. No, thanks, I'm _____ to shellfish.
8. Luckily, the fireman knew _____ and saved him.
10. For minor things, I do not to take _____. I prefer to get better on my own.
11. After that marathon, I was _____ for a week.
13. I hope he can give me pills. I hate to get a _____. I hate needles. And pain. And math tests.

DOWN

1. I slid down the rope too fast and got a _____.
3. This cut is deep and long. You'll need _____.
4. You have a high _____. Stay home and rest.
6. I wore _____ all though middle school. I hated them. But now I'm glad my smile is nicer.
9. Poor thing. Obesity _____ in his family.
10. Whoa. I spun around too many times. I'm _____.
12. I went walking through the woods and came back with a _____ on my arm. It itches a lot.

62

LONGER & SMOOTHER SPEAKING

Write about health and fitness.

If you get sick while abroad, being able to talk about health will be important.

I'm usually pretty healthy. I don't catch colds often, but when I do, they're usually bad <u>colds</u>. Sometimes I have to go to the doctor and miss school. That happens about once a year, usually at the beginning of winter. I was in a car accident last year and got a cut on my head. I needed <u>stitches</u>, but my hair hides the <u>scar</u>. That was the only time I have been to the emergency room in my life. That place was stressful. Since then, I've tried to stay healthy to avoid hospitals. About once a month I have a hangover, but I don't think that qualifies as an illness.

My parents believe in preventing illness rather than treating it. My mom fixes us healthy, well-balanced meals, and she gives us spending money so that we eat right at school and do not have to eat ramyeon or kimbap every day. My father used to jog all the time, but his knees now hurt him, so he swims or walks on a treadmill. My mom goes with him to the health club and does Pilates and yoga while he works out with weights. I think the health club is kind of where they socialize. They go there for fitness and to meet their friends. And I guess having good friends is good for your health also.

You could type it on computer and tape it above. This would check your spelling and grammar! Cool.

Conversation Station

> **But hey, first, what about some current events?**
> What did you do last night?   Last weekend?   Last summer vacation?
> What will you do after class?   Tonight?   This weekend?   This winter vacation?

Ask any question and start a conversation. Ask any group of questions. Or use the die.

Do you . . .
1. Take vitamins every day?
2. Use Chinese medicine?
3. Drink coffee to study?
4. Drink alcohol to be sociable?
5. Believe in blood type characteristics?

Are you . . .
1. Allergic to anything?
2. On a diet now? Hungry now?
3. A vegetarian? A health nut?
4. Sleepy now?
5. Taking any medicine now?

Have you ever . . .
1. Broken a bone or gotten burned?
2. Gotten cut and needed stitches?
3. Missed school because you were sick?
4. Lied about your health to skip school?
5. Saved a person's life?

Have you ever . . .
1. Fainted or passed out?
2. Been in a car accident? Train? Bus?
3. Used your phone in an emergency?
4. Had an operation? Tonsils?
5. Helped a sick or injured person?

What time . . .
1. Do you usually wake up? Go to bed?
2. Do you wake up on Saturday? Sunday?
3. Is your best time to study?
4. Do you go to bed on Saturday night?
5. Do you start classes?

When was the last time you . . .
1. Had a health checkup?
2. Exercised?
3. Caught a cold? Had a sinus allergy?
4. Went to the hospital, for any reason?
5. Went to school while sick?

 Remember, conversation is KING. If a conversation starts, go with it.

> Really?   You're kidding.   No kidding.   No way.   Say what?   Bummer.   Me too.
> Where?   When?   Why?   Who?   What time?   How?   How long?   How often?
> Kind of.   Sort of.   Sometimes.   Half and half.   It depends.

What about you?

HEALTH FREQUENCY

HOMEWORK: Fill in the blanks with your answers. For example, look at question 1. If you play a team sport once a week, write 7. Then put the total below.

CLASSWORK: You and your partner will interview each other. When you answer, try to use a phrase in regular type and a *phrase in italics*. But if a conversation starts, GO with it.

Brad	How often do you play a team sport?
Britney	Hah! *When pigs fly.* What about you?
Brad	Pretty often. *We have soccer practice twice a week.*
Britney	Really? Well, how often do you drink alcohol?
Brad	Too often. *Maybe three times a week.* What about you?
Britney	Every now and then—*mabye once a month.*
Brad	No way. How often do you like to meet your friends?
Britney	Every chance I get. *But never on Sunday.*

If you do something often, it's important to you.

So *How often do you . . . ?* is a great question for finding what's important to your partner.

Use the die, or not.

HOW OFTEN DO YOU . . . ?

#	Question			#	Question		
1	Play a team sport?	7			Eat too much?	10	
2	Have an allergy act up?	1	**1**		Drink too much?	10	**2**
3	Use Chinese medicine?	4			Get home after midnight?	8	
4	Feel great?	1			Eat after midnight?	7	
5	Wake up?	10			Eat fast food? (Burger King, Popeye's, McDonald's)	5	
6	Wake up in class?	3	**3**		Eat junk food: (chocolate, candy, pastry or chips)	7	
7	Make your bed?	5			Drink coffee?	10	**4**
8	Clean your room?	1			Drink alcohol?	7	
9	Get a heath checkup? (body, eye, teeth)	6			Take a two-hour nap?	9	
10	Exercise?	2	**5**		Wake up after noon?	6	**6**
11	Catch a cold?	4			Watch TV for four hours?	10	
12	Work out in a health club?	1			Go on a diet?	4	
	Total	45			Total	93	

Yipes!

What about you?

1	2	3	4	5
never, never ever *when pigs fly*	hardly ever *once a year*	rarely, very seldom *twice a year*	not too often *every other month*	every now and then *once a month*
6	**7**	**8**	**9**	**10**
sometimes *twice a month*	usually, generally *once a week*	frequently, often *twice a week*	every chance I get *three times a week*	all the time *100 times a day*

Really? No kidding?	Say what? No way.	Me too. Same here.	Where? When?
Wow. Great. Cool.	In your dreams.	Ditto.	Who? Why?
Awesome.	You're pulling my leg.	My father also.	What time?

65

7 Holidays, Festivals, & Feelings

Scan and find the tracks.

 37 **Vocabulary Vitamins**

HAPPY to MAD I'm:	HAPPY to SAD I was:	CALM to NERVOUS I'm:	QUALITY The festival was:
1 a happy camper	tickled pink	mellow	awesome
2 happy	thrilled	calm	fantastic
3 so-so	very happy	relaxed	excellent
4 annoyed	happy	anxious	great
5 aggravated	so-so	I've got butterflies.	pretty good
6 ticked off	sad	stressed	good
7 sick and tired (of)	bummed	nervous	OK; fair; so-so
8 angry	depressed	sweating it out	not too bad
9 mad (at)	I had the blues.	uptight	pretty bad; awful
10 furious	in a funk	freaked out	terrible; horrible

aggravating; irritating	성나게 하는; 약올리는	knock your socks off	아주 멋진
annoying	거슬리게 하는; 귀찮은	monotonous; tedious	지루한
anxious; nervous	신경이 곤두선	moody	침울한; 감정기복이 심한
ashamed	부끄러운; 창피한	pout	토라진
burned out	정신적으로 지친	proud, pride	자부심 있는 / 긍지
confused	당황한; 혼란한	recharged	재충전된
depressed; have the blues	우울한	relaxing	긴장을 푼
drained	완전히 지친	relieved	완화된, 안심시키는
dread	아주 무서운	revenge	복수심
embarrassed	당혹스러운	sick and tired	반복된 일에 질린
envy, envious	시기하는, 질투심 강한	soothing	달래는, 위로하는, 진정하는
exhausted	기진맥진한	stressed, stressed out	스트레스 받는, 스트레스 해소된
furious	몹시 화를 내는	temper tantrum	울화통; 짜증
grouchy; cranky	기분이 언짢은; 신경질 내는	ticked off	약간 화난
in a funk	침울한	tickled pink	매우 기쁜
jealous	질투하는	tranquil	조용한; 평온한
kick back; relax	쉬다	Yuck! Gross!	징그러워!

CONVERSATION STARTERS

1. **When is your birthday?** *What did you do on your last birthday?*
   My birthday is on Christmas, so I get only half as many presents as my brother. Bummer.

   _____

2. **Are birthdays big in your family?** *What did your parents give you on your last birthday?*
   Birthdays are pretty big. My mom likes to bake and to take photos, so birthdays are perfect for her.

   _____

3. **What do your parents do on their anniversary?** *For each other's birthday?*
   My father is the romantic type, so they always do something special. He likes to surprise her.

   _____

4. **Do you like going to weddings?** *Does your mother drag you to weddings of distant cousins?*
   I like weddings. It's fun to listen to the old ladies gossip about the bride.

   _____

5. **What is your favorite theme park?** *What is your favorite part?*
   I like Caribbean Bay. That new wave machine will knock your socks off. Literally.

   _____

6. **What is your favorite holiday?** *Where does your family go for Chuseok?*
   My favorite holiday is the Lunar New Year. My father is big on going to the east coast to see the sunrise.

   _____

7. **Have you been to Nami Island?** *To the east coast for the sunrise?*
   We went to Nami Island last year. It was beautiful. I got lost, but it was an island.

   _____

8. **Do you prefer to go out with one or two friends, or the more the merrier?**
   I prefer one or two friends. More than that and it's like herding cats—too hard to get everyone to decide.

   _____

Really?	No kidding.	No way!	Me too!	Bummer.	Anyway.
Kind of.	Half and half.	Sometimes.	It depends.	For example?	
Where?	When?	Why?	Who?	How?	What time?	How often?

What about you?

CONVERSATION STARTERS

9. **What will you do this winter vacation?** *Will you travel? Work? Study TV programs? (Joke.)*
   I have tentative plans to travel to Canada in February if I can make some money in January.

   _____

10. **Do you know your schedule for next semester?** *Do you have a minor or double major?*
    My schedule is not determined yet. A lot depends on my grades, so I'm keeping my fingers crossed.

    _____

11. **What is the most recent festival or theme park or ball game you've been to?**
    Last month, I went to the fireworks festival on Yeouido. It was so crowded.

    _____

12. **Did you get or give something on Valentine's Day?** *White Day? Teacher's Day?*
    Every Teacher's Day, I want to give a present to teachers who gave me an A+. I just never make an A+.

    _____

13. **What is your favorite festival?** *Festival food? What festivals have you been to recently?*
    I like the Buddha Festival and parade from Dongguk to downtown. I just love the colors.

    _____

14. **Do you prefer summer or winter parks?** *Which is your favorite? How often do you go?*
    Both. Whatever. Get me out the house. Well, the winter parks because I like snowboarding.

    _____

15. **Have you ever been to a costume party?** *What did you go as?*
    Last semester, my major department had a costume party. I went as Spider-Man, so I got really thirsty.*

    _____

16. **Does your father like to do something or nothing on holidays?**
    My father used to be an action addict—big camping trips or whatever. Now he likes to stay home.

    _____

Write your own question: _____

Really?	No kidding?	No way!	Me too!	Bummer.	Anyway.
It depends.	For example?	Where?	When?	Why?	Who?	How?	How often?

* The Spider-Man mask has no opening for the mouth.

What about you?

MODEL CONVERSATION

Brad   Hey, Britney. How was your three-day weekend?

Britney   <u>Awesome</u>. We went to Everland.

Brad   I've been there. That place is fantastic.

Britney   Yeah. Well, originally, my father wanted a <u>tranquil</u> weekend, but my sister and I got him to go for an exciting weekend.

Brad   Did your sister have fun too?

Britney   Eventually. We left early in the morning, and she is always <u>cranky</u> when she gets up early, so that was a pain.

Brad   How long was she <u>grouchy</u>?

Britney   Not long. As soon as she saw the entrance sign, she turned into a <u>happy camper</u>.

Brad   What was your favorite part of Everland?

Britney   Oh, the Tornado Roller Coaster. It'll <u>knock your socks off</u>. Talk about thrilling!

Brad   Did your mother ride it?

Britney   No way. She gets <u>nervous</u> on a glass elevator. But my sister screamed till tears came out of her eyes.

Brad   What about your father?

Britney   He's <u>game for anything</u>. He's an action addict. He was a paratrooper when he was in the army.

Brad   I wish my dad were the outdoors type. He just wants to <u>kick back</u> and <u>relax</u> every weekend.

Britney   What did you do over the holidays?

Brad   Oh, I studied. My mother said she was <u>sick and tired</u> of my coming home late and getting low grades.

Britney   Ouch. So your mom is the <u>bad cop</u>?

Brad   Yeah. Frankly, I was kind of relieved when the holiday was over so I could come back to school.

Britney   You amaze me. Your dad didn't say anything?

Brad   No, he was asleep on the sofa. Or <u>playing possum</u>. He's pretty <u>mellow</u>. Frankly, I think he's given up on me.

Britney   You'll impress him someday. You're just a late bloomer.

Brad   What's that?

Britney   Some flowers or plants start to grow late, but they end up OK.

Brad   Yeah, yeah, that's me. Bloomin' Brad! I like it.

Her boyfriend just struck out, so she is bummed out.

Put a check next to the festivals and parks you have been to. ✓

FESTIVALS
- Andong Mask Dance
- Bongpyeong Cultural
- Boryeong Mud
- Boseong Green Tea
- Busan Film
- Cheongdo Bullfighting
- Damyang Bamboo
- Hampyeong Butterfly
- Icheon Ceramic
- Jarasum Jazz
- Jindo Sea Parting
- Jinju Lantern
- Mountain Trout Ice
- Muju Firefly
- Seoul Fireworks

THEME PARKS
- Children's Grand Park
- Everland
- Gyeongju World
- Lotte World
- Me World
- Pyeong Hwa Land
- Seoul Land
- Woobang Land

WATER PARKS
- Blue Canyon
- California Beach
- Caribbean Bay
- Four Seasons
- Ocean World
- Onemount
- Peak Island
- Tedin Waterpark & Spa

Rank your favorites (1, 2, 3) here.

TOP 5 CULTURAL DIFFERENCES

These cultural differences can also be conversation starters. You can ask:
What do you think about number 1? How do you feel about number 2? Which way do you prefer?

1. Americans get older on their birthday, but Koreans change their age on Lunar New Year's Day.
2. In Korea, on your birthday you usually pay if you go out with your friends. In America, you never pay on your birthday—your friends do.
3. Christmas in America is a family holiday, whereas in Korea it is more of a dating or couples' holiday.
4. Most American towns have their own unique festival or annual celebration, and these almost always include a parade.
5. Korea has Coming-of-Age Day (성년의 날) and 100-day parties for babies. America has neither.

NATIONAL HOLIDAYS
New Year's Day
Independence Movement Day
Children's Day
Buddha's Birthday
Memorial Day
Liberation Day
Chuseok
National Foundation Day
Christmas Day

CULTURE QUESTIONS
Many Korean cities are developing and promoting their own theme festivals to attract tourism.
Is this an effective use of city funds?
If you could create a festival for your hometown, what would it be?
What do you think of Coming-of-Age Day? Is it becoming extinct? Did you dress up and celebrate?

VOCABULARY DEVELOPMENT

ACROSS
1. Her dog ran away, and her boyfriend's in the army. She's got the _____.
3. I am _____ after that test. I need a beer.
4. I'm burned _____ after seven midterm tests.
7. My mom was _____ when I got a scholarship.
9. And my grandmother was _____ pink.
12. His parents were really _____ when he was kicked out of school for cheating.
13. You told the teacher I missed class because I went to Everland? I'll get _____. Soon.

DOWN
1. I still get _____ before every speech.
2. Don't _____. Maybe you'll pass the next test.
5. That spoiled rich kid had a temper _____.
6. You're just _____ because the teacher gives me more attention.
8. She got _____ when the professor wouldn't accept her late homework.
10. She's fun to be around, always a happy _____.
11. I _____ telling my parents that I flunked out.

LONGER & SMOOTHER SPEAKING

Write about your favorite holiday, festival, or birthday.

My favorite holiday is Christmas because my parents are really into it. When I was young, my father would always dress up as Santa and come in the front door and give presents, yelling, "Ho, ho, ho!" Of course, at the time I didn't know that was my dad. Mom is a great actress. She would act so surprised. My little sister would cry and scream in fear, and I would just run straight to the presents. So I have great memories of Christmas.

My favorite festival is the Jindo Sea Parting Festival. That is just so neat the way the sea parts. I've been there four times, and it was <u>awesome</u> every time. We stay at the same place every time, and it has a great view. These days, it's getting commercialized and overcrowded. In France, there is a place called Mont St. Michel where the same thing happens. My dream is to go there.

My favorite birthday was last year. My birthday and high school graduation were on the same day, so I was one <u>happy camper</u>. We went out to eat with all my grandparents and took a bunch of pictures. That was the last time that I spent with all four of them, so those pictures are very special. They were all very proud that I got into a good university. And they all gave me money. Love and soju flowed that night!

You could type it on computer and tape it above. This would check your spelling and grammar! Cool.

CONVERSATION

But first! Look at the list of festivals on page 63. Find five festivals that you and your partner:
A) have gone to. B) have not gone to. C) want to go to. Make a list.

Who gives you more stress . . .
1. Your father or mother?
2. Your friends or family?
3. Your older or younger sibling?
4. Your mother's or father's parents?

What is your favorite . . .
1. Holiday? Water park?
2. Festival in Seoul? Nature festival?
3. Festival outside of Seoul?
4. Winter festival? Summer festival?

How was . . .
1. Your first puppy love?
2. Your last birthday?
3. Last weekend? Last night?
4. Last summer vacation? Winter?

Where is your favorite . . .
1. Place to relax? Place to party?
2. Place to study? Place to shop?
3. Place to hang out?
4. Place to drink? Drink coffee?

Have you ever . . .
1. Seen the sunrise on the east coast?
2. Climbed Hallasan to the top?
3. Gone to Jongro for New Year's Eve?
4. Seen the Buddha Lantern Parade?

What was your . . .
1. Best birthday? Worst birthday?
2. Favorite subject in high school?
3. Scariest moment?
4. Most embarrassing moment?

HAPPY to MAD
1. **happy camper** No problem. I'm a happy camper.
2. **happy** I got an A+. I was happy about that.
3. **OK** I felt OK, but wish I had scored higher.
4. **annoyed** He kept annoying me. I was annoyed.
5. **aggravated** He's aggravating me. I am aggravated.
6. **ticked off** He ticked me off. I was ticked off.
7. **sick and tired** I'm sick and tired of your being late.
8. **mad** Yes, I'm mad! I'm mad at you, dummy.
9. **furious** I was furious. I was furious at her.

HAPPY to SAD
1. **tickled pink** I was tickled pink when I got accepted.
2. **thrilled** They were thrilled when I won.
3. **very happy** I'm very happy with my major.
4. **so-so** I felt so-so when I came in second to last.
5. **sad** I was sad when he went into the army.
6. **bummed** An F! Bummer. I'm bummed out.
7. **depressed** I'm depressed. Your story is too depressing.
8. **blue** I was blue for two weeks after we broke up.
9. **have (got) the blues** He flunked. He's got the blues.

Really?   You're kidding.   No way!   Say what?   Me too!   Bummer.
Where?   When?   Why?   Who?   What time?   How?   How long?   How often?
Kind of.   Sort of.   Sometimes.   Half and half.   It depends.   For example?

STATION

Ask any question and start a conversation. Ask any group of questions. Or use the die.

Have you ever . . . ?
1. Gone to a Halloween party?
2. Gone to a surprise party?
3. Gone to a costume party?
4. Gone to TGIF's on your birthday?

4

What is your favorite . . . ?
1. Theme park? Ethnic food?
2. Mountain to climb?
3. Festival? Festival food?
4. Beach? Place to ski?

What kind of . . .
1. Music do you hate? Movies?
2. Commercials do you hate?
3. TV programs do you hate?
4. Required classes do you hate?

5

When was the last time you . . . ?
1. Were embarrassed?
2. Got praise from your parents?
3. Got a compliment from a teacher?
4. Gave someone a compliment?

When is the last time you . . .
1. Went to a party with your major?
2. Went to a water park? Ski resort?
3. Went to Hyewha? Hongdae?
4. Got up to let an old person sit?

6

Do you . . .
1. Complain when you get a low grade?
2. Get nervous before a presentation?
3. Buy expensive birthday presents?
4. Tell white lies to get more allowance?

CALM to NERVOUS
1. **mellow** He's so mellow that nothing bothers him.
2. **calm** How can you be so calm before your speech?
3. **relaxed** I was relaxed because I was well prepared.
4. **anxious** I'm always anxious before I get a test back.
5. **butterflies** I had butterflies in my stomach.
6. **nervous** I was nervous before the final exam.
7. **stressed** I was stressed from all those final exams.
8. **nervous wreck** I was a nervous wreck before my speech.
9. **freaked out** I freaked out when my food started moving.

QUALITY, FROM AWESOME to AWFUL
That festival was . . . My birthday was . . .
1. awesome, fantastic
2. superb, excellent, outstanding
3. very good
4. so-so, OK, fair
5. not too good, you didn't miss a thing, no smash hit
6. bad
7. awful, terrible, horrible
8. the pits, it stank, yuck

What about you?

8 WORKING & GETTING THERE

Scan and find the tracks.

Whoa. I think he's had enough coffee already.

Maybe we should try to fix her up with the coffee guy?

He wishes he had studied harder in college.

 42

VOCABULARY VITAMINS

PERSONALITY OPPOSITES

boss from hell	최악의 직장상사	pushover	호락호락한 상사	**IDIOMS**
boss's pet	상사의 총애를 받는 사람	in the doghouse	난처한 입장에 처한; 미움 사게 된	**WORKPLACE RANKING**
brownnose	아첨꾼	badmouth	헐뜯는 사람	flunky; gofer
goes by the book	매뉴얼을 따르다	loose cannon	돌발행동을 하는 사람	grunt
career track	경력 쌓는 길	mommy track	여성의 승진 탈락	suit
company man	회사원	entrepreneur	사업가	big boss; top dog
happy camper	즐기는 사람	moody; malcontent	기분 변화가 심한; 불평하는 사람	**MANAGEMENT STYLES**
have your act together	정리를 하다	disorganized	체계적이지 않은 사람	carrot and stick
idea person	아이디어를 잘 생각해 내는 사람	detail person	꼼꼼한 사람	hands-on / hands-off
lone wolf	혼자서 일을 잘 처리하는	team player	협업을 잘하는	**COMMUNICATION**
people person	사교적인	anti-social; hermit	은둔하는	networking
queen bee	지시하는 사람	worker bee	일만하는 사람	on the same page
self-starter	자발적으로 행동하는 사람	watch the clock	퇴근 시간만 기다리다	**INDEPENDENT**
top dog	상사	low man on the totem pole	말단 사원	entrepreneur
workaholic	일벌레	slacker	게으름뱅이	freelance
				self-employed

highway	큰 도로 (예:서울~의정부)	intersection	교차로
expressway	고속도로	lost	길을 잃은
breakdown	고장난	main drag	도시 중심가
bridge	다리	map	지도
bumper-to-bumper traffic	교통체증이 심한	ride shotgun	앞좌석에 앉다
bus lane / fast lane	버스 전용 도로 / 추월차선	rush hour	교통혼잡 시간대
commute	통근하다	shortcut	지름길
designated driver	술 마시지 않도록 지정된 운전자	shuttle bus	셔틀버스
DWI (driving while intoxicated)	음주운전	toll booth / toll road	통행료 내는 곳 / 유료도로
fender bender	경미한 차량 사고	totaled	자동차가 완전히 망가진
flat tire	바람 빠진 타이어	traffic jam	교통체증
gas (gasoline) / diesel	가솔린 / 디젤	traffic ticket	교통위반 딱지
gas guzzler	기름을 많이 소모하는 차	transfer	환승
GPS	내비게이션	underground parking	지하 주차장
hand-me-down car	물려받은 오래된 자동차	walking distance	도보거리
hitchhike	여행 중 남의 차 얻어타기	wreck; accident	교통사고

CONVERSATION STARTERS

1. **Have you ever had a part-time job?** *What about a full-time job during the semester break?*
   Every weekend, I help my mother—she owns a coffee shop. One summer, I did telemarketing.

   _____

2. **What does your father do?** *Does he do any work at home on the weekends?*
   My father works at a bank. He is the personnel manager. Every now and then, he works at home.

   _____

3. **Does your mother work?** *Is she on the career track or the mommy track?*
   My mother is a pharmacist and works part-time. So I guess that is the mommy track.

   _____

4. **Do you want to follow the career track or the mommy track?** *What about your future wife?*
   I'd like to follow the career track to make money until we have a baby, and then work part-time.

   _____

5. **Do your parents have easy or stressful jobs?** *Are they home for supper every night?*
   My father is a high school principal, so he gives stress, I think. He's home for supper most nights.

   _____

6. **Has your father or mother ever changed jobs?** *Would they like to?*
   My father moved from Samsung to LG. They made him a great offer. Now he's a boss.

   _____

7. **What does your father or mother like most about their job?** *Dislike the most?*
   My mother works for Korean Airlines, and she gets to travel for free a lot. She likes that.

   _____

8. **What is your dream job?** *Is it realistic?*
   My dream job is to be a movie translator. Realistically, I'll probably work at my father's company.

   _____

Really?	*No kidding?*	*No way!*	*Me too!*	*Bummer.*	*Anyway.*
Kind of.	*Half and half.*	*Sometimes.*	*It depends.*	*For example?*	
Where?	*When?*	*Why?*	*Who?*	*How?*	*What time?*	*How often?*

What about you?

CONVERSATION STARTERS  44

9. **Do your parents drive to work?** *Do they like to drive?*
   My dad drives to work. He leaves early in the morning to beat the rush hour.
   _____

10. **Where do you live?** *How do you get to school? Do you have a driver's license?*
    I live in Bundang and get to school by subway and bus. I'll get my license this winter.
    _____

11. **How much do you spend every week on transportation?** *How many hours per week?*
    Well, $3 a day for five days is $15. Every week, I spend ten hours on the subway.
    _____

12. **Have you ever fallen asleep and missed your subway stop?** *How many times?*
    That happened last week. Luckily, one of my neighbors recognized me and woke me up.
    _____

13. **Have you ever been in an car, bus, or train accident?** *Ever used your phone in an emergency?*
    I was in a minor accident when I was 8, and I saw a bus slide off the road last winter.
    _____

14. **Are family vacations in the car fun or tiring?**
    They start out fun but end up tiring. Once, for Chuseok, we were in the car for twelve hours.
    _____

15. **Does your father or mother travel a lot for work?** *Overseas? Where? For how long?*
    My father is a regional manager, so he travels all over the province. He goes to China once a year.
    _____

16. **If you could have any kind of car, what would it be?** *German? American? What color?*
    I'd like a four-door, midnight-blue BMW. That's my dream car.
    _____

Write your own question: _____

| Really? | No kidding? | No way! | Me too! | Bummer. | Anyway. |
| It depends. | For example? | Where? | When? | Why? | Who? | How? | How often? |

What about you?

76

MODEL CONVERSATION

Britney Hey, Brad. How was your weekend?

Brad Exhausting. It's ironic. I'm super busy on the weekends, and I recharge my batteries during the week.

Britney You poor thing.

Brad Enough sarcasm.

Britney Sorry. So, again, how was your weekend?

Brad Well, you know I have a part-time job with my uncle on Saturdays. I like working for him, but his office is so far away, it takes over an hour by subway to get there.

Britney Bummer. You commute to school during the week and to work on the weekends.

Brad Yeah. He's offered to pay for a taxi, but the traffic is bumper to bumper in Gangnam, so I wouldn't save any time.

Britney You ever think of getting a driver's license?

Brad My uncle wants me to. I could show American clients around and translate for them.

Britney Wow. Sounds like you have a future with your uncle's company.

Brad We'll see. Driving and speaking English—talk about multi-tasking!

Britney You can do it, Brad. You're the man!

Brad Thanks.

Britney Do you like the guys who work for your uncle?

Brad Yeah, they're all hard-working self-starters. Not a slacker in the bunch. Well, his daughter, my first cousin is, well . . . No, this is the new me. I'm not going to badmouth my boss's daughter.

Britney Good idea. Is your uncle a nice boss?

Brad Oh yeah, he's a pushover. He's hands-off and doesn't micro-manage.

Britney Is he a workaholic?

Brad Yes, but it's his company. He's an entrepreneur and a self-made man. Say, after you graduate, you might be a good fit for his company.

Britney Really? Why do you say that?

Brad You're a detail person, and that's one thing his company lacks. Do you plan on following the career track or the mommy track?

Britney I want to follow the money track. I want my own money so I can marry for love and not for financial security.

Brad Sounds like you've given it a lot of thought.

Britney Like you said, I'm a detail person.

They look like team players, but maybe it's a love triangle?

77

TOP 5 CULTURAL DIFFERENCES

These cultural differences can also be conversation starters. You can ask:
What do you think about number 1? How do you feel about number 2? Which way do you prefer?

1. Americans change jobs more often than Koreans do and have less company loyalty.
2. Americans usually do not wear uniforms in places like banks, as Koreans often do.
3. If necessary, Koreans are expected to work as many hours as necessary, no matter how late at night, without extra pay. If American hourly workers work extra hours, they get paid at higher rates.
4. Korea has designated driver companies, but America does not.
5. Koreans do not like 3D work (dirty, dangerous, and difficult). In America, 3D workers and skilled manual laborers often are paid well and are socially valued for their skills. (A good plumber or carpenter can often make as much as a professor.)

That's called 'watching the clock.'

CULTURE QUESTIONS
Would you prefer to have a nice, modern apartment outside of Seoul and a long commute, or to have an older apartment in the center of Seoul?
Many Koreans workers don't leave work until their boss does. Is this fair, or has it become an old-fashioned concept?

VOCABULARY DEVELOPMENT

ACROSS
1. I was hired last week. I'm the low man on the _____ pole.
5. You shouldn't _____ your boss to his secretary.
6. Sorry I'm late. I was caught in _____ hour traffic.
9. He always has lunch by himself. He's a _____ wolf.
10. He's a _____. Every day he's first in and last out.
13. I'll follow the _____ track until I have a baby.
14. Ask Jack to proofread this. He's a _____ person.
15. You got a traffic _____? Bummer.

DOWN
2. I _____ at Dongdaemun. What about you?
3. You call yourself an executive assistant? You're just a well-dressed _____.
4. He's a great people _____. He should be in sales.
7. He's too lazy to even look for a job. What a _____.
8. There was an accident on the bridge and _____ was all backed up.
11. Once a year we all have to check inventory. I hate that _____ work.
12. She's an _____ person and very creative. She should be in advertising.

LONGER & SMOOTHER SPEAKING

Write about your father or mother's job, or your part-time job.
Or write about all three.

My father is a branch manager for Kookmin Bank. He's a <u>company man</u>, and he's worked for them for twenty years. He has great loyalty to them. Every now and then, another bank will wine and dine him to try to hire him, but he never leaves. He says banking is easy, people are hard. He's a real <u>people person</u>, and a big part of his job is keeping the workers happy and their morale up. He remembers when he was the <u>low man on the totem pole</u>, so he shows extra attention to the new workers.

My mom, on the other hand, is an <u>entrepreneur</u>. She worked for a company for about three years, learned all she could, and then started her own company. Right now, she runs three small companies, and she's working at a real-estate office to learn that business. She is definitely on the <u>career path</u>. She would be bored staying home and cleaning the house.

I've had two part-time jobs in my life. Last summer, I tutored two neighborhood kids in math while they were preparing for the university entrance exams. That job was OK, but I spent more time making them behave than I did teaching math. Sometimes I felt like I was just a glorified babysitter. But the money was good. Now I work at a 7-11, and that is low stress. And low pay.

You could type it on computer and tape it above. This would check your spelling and grammar! Cool.

CONVERSATION

Open your book. Your partner closes their book.
Turn the book sideways to that you can see this page and your partner can see the other page.
Nobody can see their partner's questions.

1

Are you a self-starter or a slacker?
Have you ever been fired?
Fired by a relative?

Do you use a neighborhood shuttle bus?
How far is the subway station from your house?

Does your father drive to work?
How long does it take?
What kind of car does he have?

Is your father a joiner or a loner?
Does he have drinking buddies? Fishing buddies? Golf buddies?

3

How did you get your part-time job?
Family connections?
Did you have a job interview?

Is your father a detail person or an idea person?
Is he a boss?
Is his desk at home neat?

If your father could start his own business, what kind would it be?
If your mother could start...?
If you could start....?

What time does your father get home every night?
Do you have supper together?
Would you like to?

5

Would you like the same career as your father? Mother?
Will you ever take over the family business?

Where do you live?
How do you get to school?
How long does it take?
Do you want to live in the dormitory?

Have you ever met your father's boss? Your mother's boss?
Oh, your mother is the boss?

Have you ever gone to work with your father and seen exactly what he does?
How old were you?
Were you impressed?

Really? No kidding? Say what? Me too! Bummer.
Where? When? Why? Who? How? How long? How often?
Kind of.   Sometimes.   Half and half.   It depends.

What about you?

80

STATION

Ask any question and start a conversation. Ask any group of questions.
Or use the die. It it lands with 3 up, ask a 3 question. Talk about all the 3 questions, or roll again.
This is not interview class. It's conversation class. When a conversation starts, *go go go*.

6

Do you have a driver's license?
When do you plan on getting it?
Do you think it will be easy or difficult?

Have you ever ridden a motorcycle?
Are you an action addict? Adrenaline junkie? Wannabe?

What is the best part of your part-time job? The worst part?
How many hours do you work per week? On what days?

Does your father like his job? Your mother?
Do you like your major?
Do you like this class?

4

Does your father want you to study harder so you will have a better job than his?
What did your grandfathers do?

Has your father ever changed jobs? Your mother?
Has your family moved?
Which town do you like better?

Would you rather have a high-paying stressful job, or a lower-paying fun job?
Would you like to be idle rich?

If you could have any kind of car, what would it be?
Does your father work on his car?
Have you ever driven his car?
Ever washed it?

2

Have you ever had a part-time job?
Have you ever tutored a student?
Did you get fired because their grades did not improve?

Is your father a company man or an entrepreneur?
Is your father a boss?
At work, does he give stress or get stress?

What is your dream job?
What is your realistic job?
What kind of job would you *never* do?

Does your father socialize with the people at work?
(Does he hang out with them away from work?)

What about you?

Really? No kidding No way Say what? Me too! Bummer.
Where? When? Why? Who? How? How long? How often?
Kind of sometimes half and half it depends

81

9 PRONUNCIATION PRACTICE

Koreans have trouble with these sounds, so here is some practice.
ㅂ, ㅍ = B, P, V, F, Ph   ㄹ = L, N, R   ㅈ, ㅊ = CH, J, G, Z   ㅌ = T, TH

You can go to the website *jazzenglish.com* and listen to the pronunciation of these words.

1 FIRST GROUP

	1st	2nd	3rd	4th
1	lack	rack	nack	wack
2	late	rate	wait	Nate
3	lay	ray	way	nay
4	bail	pale	fail	veil
5	bane	pane	feign	vain
6	bill	pill	fill	vill
7	bead	bad	bed	bid
8	beat	bat	bet	bit
9	cheat	chat	Chet	chit
10	meet	mat	met	mitt
11	sheer	cheer	shin	chin
12	lead	read	need	weed
13	led	red	Ned	wed
14	bare	pair	fare	vair
15	base	pace	face	vase
16	Bast	past	fast	vast
17	deed	dad	dead	did
18	eat	at	et	it
19	feast	fast	fest	fist
20	pool	pull	Paul	pole

Pant. That's enough for today.

2

	1st	2nd	3rd	4th
21	feed	fad	fed	fid
22	feet	fat	fet	fit
23	leel	real	kneel	wheel
24	leer	near	rear	we're
25	least	last	lest	list
26	bat	pat	fat	vat
27	bowl	foal	pole	vole
28	beel	peel	feel	veal
29	bye	pie	fie	vie
30	soon	sun	sawn	sewn
31	gin	chin	zen	shin
32	Jane	chain	Zane	Shane
33	gyp	chip	zip	ship
34	life	rife	knife	wife
35	light	right	night	white
36	doon	done	Don	dawn
37	beer	peer	fear	veer
38	berry	Perry	ferry	very
39	ban	pan	fan	van
40	bent	pent	fent	vent

3 SECOND GROUP

	1st	2nd	3rd	4th
41	sheep	cheap	ship	chip
42	he'd	had	head	hid
43	heat	hat	het	hit
44	lip	rip	nip	whip
45	lock	rock	knock	wok
46	low	row	no	woe
47	neat	Nat	net	knit
48	peat	pat	pet	pit
49	reed	rad	red	rid
50	bile	pile	file	vile
51	bine	pine	fine	vine
52	by	pie	phi	vie
53	seat	sat	set	sit
54	seed	sad	said	Sid
55	seen	san	sen	sin
56	sap	zap	jap	chap
57	Jew	chew	zoo	shoe
58	Joe	Cho	Zoh	show
59	lead	lad	led	lid
60	boor	poor	four	for

4

	1st	2nd	3rd	4th
61	noon	none	noun	known
62	Rhine	wine	nine	line
63	fool	full	foul	foal
64	link	rink	wink	
65	teen	tan	tin	
66	wheel	well	will	
67	lake	rake	wake	
68	letter	wetter	redder	
69	boom	bum	bomb	
70	goon	gun	gone	
71	lewd	rude	nude	
72	lice	rice	nice	
73	rail	nail	wail	
74	bro	pro	fro	
75	bit	fit	pit	
76	meal	Mell	mill	
77	leak	week	reek	
78	fear	beer	peer	
79	beat	peat	feet	
80	bill	pill	fill	

5 THIRD GROUP

	Left	Middle	Right
81	this	tis	dis
82	though	toe	doe
83	thought	sought	taught
84	threw	true	drew
85	thy	tie	die
86	them	Tim	dim
87	theme	team	deem
88	there	tear	dare
89	therm	term	derm
90	think	tink	dink
91	loom	room	womb
92	kneel	real	wheel
93	lair	rare	where
94	cab	cap	calf
95	hoot	hut	hot
96	swab	swap	suave
97	fork	park	pork
98	wrap	lap	nap
99	raid	Wade	laid
100	toon	ton	town

6

	Left	Middle	Right
101	lent	rent	went
102	new	rue	loo
103	leather	weather	nether
104	man	mean	men
105	batter	patter	fatter
106	lather	rather	
107	legal	regal	
108	loyal	royal	
109	rational	national	
110	billow	pillow	
111	boat	vote	
112	boil	foil	
113	brown	frown	
114	razor	laser	
115	poodle	puddle	
116	list	wrist	
117	spoon	spun	
118	lighter	writer	
119	liver	river	
120	slacker	snacker	

Top 40 Konglish Expressions

Here is a list of things that Americans do not say, but Koreans think they say.
These are not necessarily bad grammar; they are just not used by Americans, or are used differently.
For example, Americans seldom begin a sentence with "Especially."

	Americans do not say	**Americans really say**
1	almost (to mean "most"/"mostly")	most of, almost always, almost everywhere
2	arbeit	part-time job
3	Are you boring?	Are you bored?
4	CF	commercial
5	cunning	cheating
6	cut the film	can't remember, blacked out
7	DC	discount
8	eat medicine	take medicine
9	especially	(Don't begin a sentence with this word.)
10	eye shopping	Browsing, window shopping
11	Fighting!	Do it! Go for it!
12	Frankly speaking, . . .	To be honest, Honestly, Frankly
13	high eyes	high standards, picky
14	How about your feelings?	How did you feel?
15	How about your weekend?	How was your weekend?
16	I envy you.	Wow! You lucky dog.
17	I have a plan this weekend.	I have plans this weekend.
18	I'm funny.	I'm having fun.
19	In my case, . . .	Just begin with *I* . . .
20	make a boyfriend or girlfriend	meet or find
21	maul bus / village bus	shuttle bus
22	meeting	blind date
23	overeat	throw up
24	play with my friends	hang out with my friends
25	pocket money	allowance, spending money
26	said to me	told me
27	salaryman	(Americans say the exact job or industry.)
28	same to me, same to her	me too, her too
29	See you again!	See you later!
30	service	freebie, on the house, complimentary
31	She has princess disease.	She's stuck-up / conceited.
32	sign	signature or autograph ("Sign" is a verb.)
33	super	supermarket, convenience store
34	take a rest	take a break
35	talent	celebrity, actor, singer, MC, host
36	This is funny.	This is fun.
37	toilet	restroom
38	vinyl house	greenhouse
39	yesterday night	last night
40	yet	not yet

STOP saying these things

10 DIRECTIONS

Scan and find the tracks.

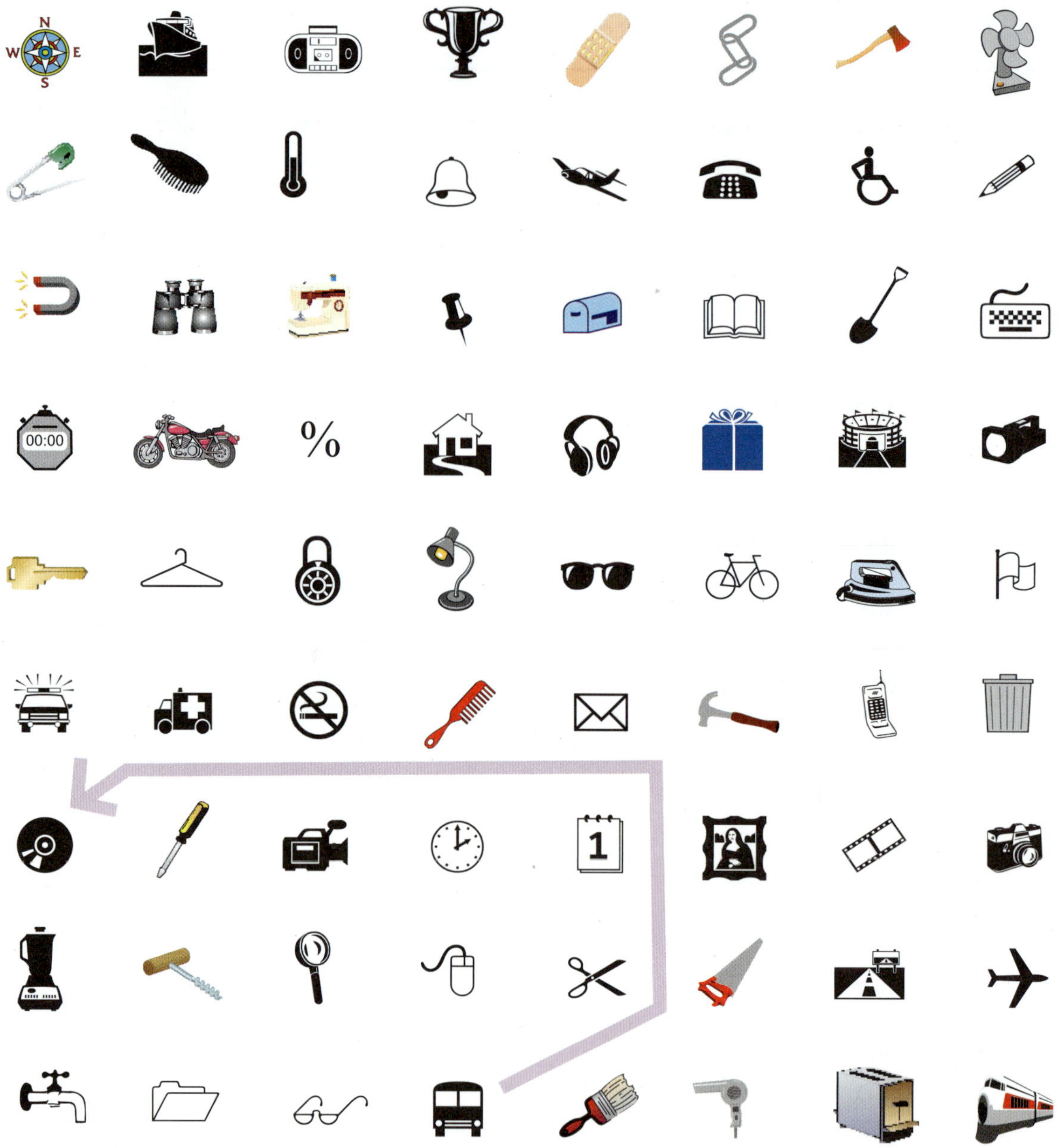

 47

compass	cruise ship	boombox	trophy	bandage	paper clips	hatchet; ax	fan
safety pin	hairbrush	thermometer	bell	plane	phone	handicap sign	pencil
magnet	binoculars	sewing machine	pushpin	mailbox	book	shovel	keyboard
stopwatch	motorcycle	percentage sign	house	earphones	present	stadium	flashlight
key	coat hanger	combination lock	lamp	sunglasses	bicycle	iron	flag
police car	ambulance	"no smoking" sign	comb	envelope	hammer	cell phone	trash can
disc	screwdriver	video camera	clock	calendar	painting	film	camera
blender	corkscrew	magnifying glass	mouse	scissors	saw	highway	jet
faucet	file folder	reading glasses	bus	paintbrush	blowdryer	toaster	train

The previous page has seventy-two icons. Why so many? Because many of them are items you use every day, such as a trash can and a comb. But you do not know the word for them in English. Thus, in this unit you will learn directions, descriptions, and vocabulary at the same time.

There are two basic types of directions:
    1) Where is something? and 2) How do you get there?

There are also two basic ways of describing something:
    1) by what it does, and 2) by what it looks like.

This unit will help you give both types of directions, and both types of descriptions. In addition, you will learn some vocabulary.

1. WHERE IS . . .?

To avoid confusion, it is always best to explain where something is in more than one way. For example: Where is North Korea? *North Korea is north of South Korea.* True. But China and Russia are also north of South Korea. Therefore, a good answer would be, *North Korea is north of South Korea* and *south of China.* Or, *North Korea is in between China and South Korea.*

Where is the mailbox?

The mailbox is above the paintbrush. True, but there are eight items above the paintbrush.

A) *The mailbox is above the earphones and below the plane.*
B) *The mailbox is in between the pushpin and the book.*
C) *The mailbox is to the right of the pushpin.*
D) *The mailbox is on the left side of the book.*

2. HOW DO I GET THERE?

An example is done for you. Follow these directions and draw a line:

How do I get to the music store? Start at the bus and go northeast in between the paint brush and the scissors. Then turn left and go north in between the scissors and the saw. Keep going north and go in between the calendar and the painting. Then turn left after the calendar and go west. Go west in between the clock and the comb, in between the video camer and the no-smoking sign, in between the screwdriver and the ambulance, and then go southwest and bam, hit the CD.

A) Now your teacher will give you directions and you will draw a line.
B) Then you and your partner will take turns. You will draw a line in your book, and then give directions to your partner, and they will draw a line in their book.
C) Then your partner will do the same and you will draw a line following your partner's directions.

3. DESCRIBING WHAT IT DOES

Describe what an object does, and your partner will guess, or ask questions and guess. For example:

A: You use it for communication.
B: The telephone! Too easy.
A: Wrong.
B: Can you carry it around with you?
A: Yes.
B: The cell phone.
A: Got it.

4. DESCRIBING WHAT IT LOOKS LIKE

A: It's long and skinny, and it's pointing toward the southwest.
B: The screwdriver.
A: No. It's not as long as the screwdriver, and it's sharp on the bottom and blunt on the top.
B: The corkscrew!
A: Du-uh. The corkscrew is pointing toward the southEAST!
B: Oh, yeah, right. Then, uh, the pencil!
A: Bingo.

STREET DIRECTIONS

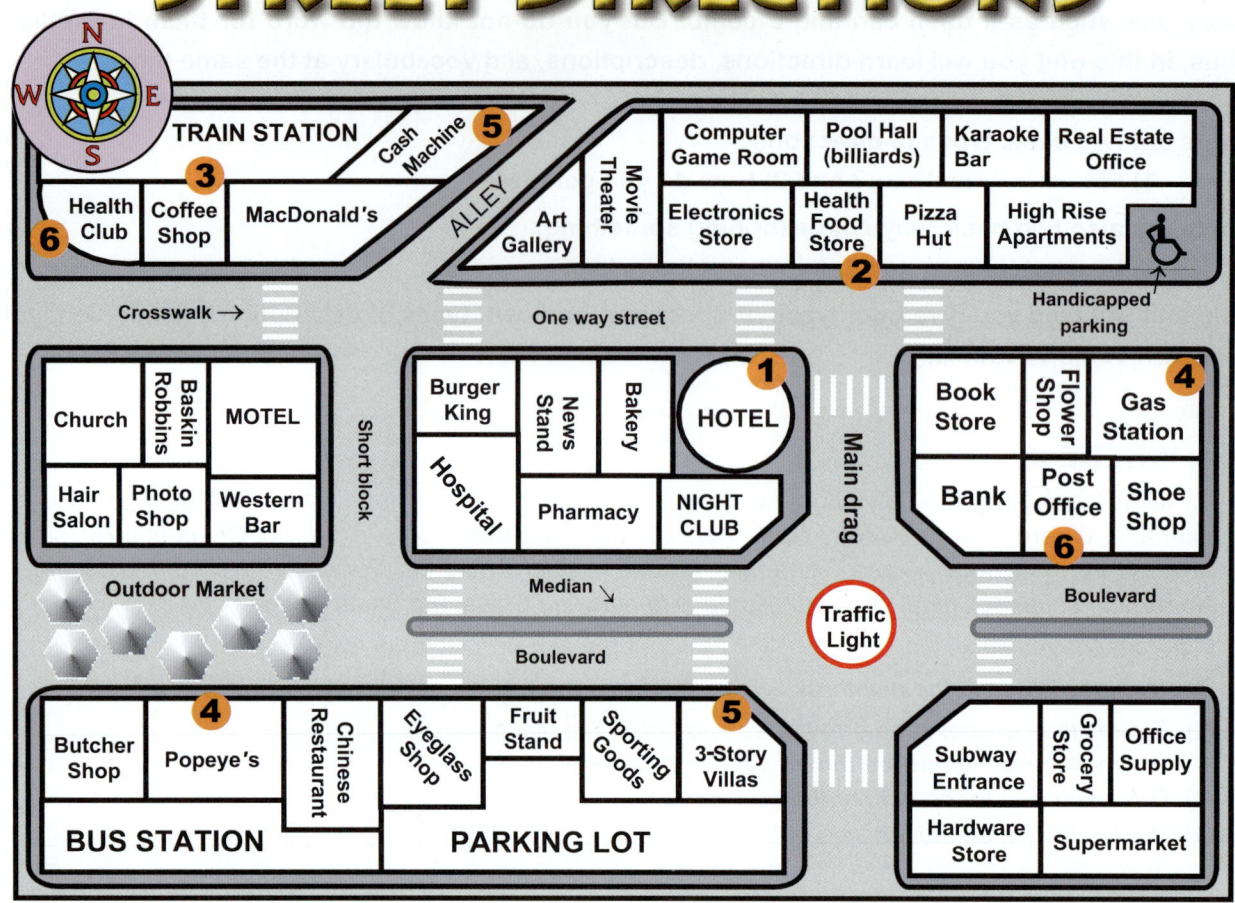

 48

BUS		DIRECTIONS		ROADS	
bus terminal	버스 터미널	above	위에	back road	뒷길 / 시골길
village bus	마을버스	on top of	맨 위에	country road	시골길
express bus	고속버스	north of	북쪽으로 (위쪽으로)	dirt road	비포장 도로
sit-down bus	좌석버스	in between	~사이에	road	길
toll booth / gate	톨게이트	in the middle	~중간에	highway	간선도로
TRAIN		in the center	~중간에	main highway	주요 간선도로
train station	기차역	next to	~옆에	expressway	고속도로
first class	일등석	on the side of	~옆에	interstate highway	주간 고속도로
second class	이등석	across from	맞은편에	alley	오솔길 / 좁은길
third class	삼등석	kitty-corner to	대각선으로	intersection	교차로
		to the right of	오른편에	3-way intersection	삼거리
SUBWAY		on the right side	오른편에	sidewalk	보도 / 인도
subway station	지하철 역	east of	동쪽으로 (오른쪽으로)	crosswalk	횡단보도
subway token	지하철 표	on the left side	왼쪽에	speed bump	과속방지 턱
ticket booth	매표소	to the left of	왼쪽에	block	블럭 (한 구획)
transfer	(교통수단을) 갈아타다	west of	서쪽으로 (왼쪽으로)	boulevard	큰길 / 대로
exit	4번 출구	below	아래로	median	중앙분리대
escalator	에스컬레이터	under	아래로	main drag	번화가
packed	사람이 꽉찬 / 만원의	south of	남쪽으로 (아래로)	elevated highway	고가도로
road construction	도로공사	in front of	~앞에	overpass	고가도로
AIRPORT		behind	~뒤에	underpass	지하도
baggage check-in	수화물 수속	in the back of	~뒤에	people overpass	육교
customs	세관	turn	도세요	bridge	다리
duty-free shop	면세점	stop	멈추세요	tunnel	터널
gate	탑승구	back up	뒤로 물러나세요	traffic jam	교통혼잡
long-term parking	장기 주차장	U-turn	유턴 (하세요)	way over there	저쪽길에
money exchange	환전				

In America, giving street directions is easier because you can use street names.

For example, go down Main Street and turn left on Park Avenue. In Korea, many street names are new and not yet well-known, so you must use landmarks, such as stores and buildings. The street map contains the names of forty-eight landmarks. Why so many? Because some of the shop names you know, such as the butcher shop, but you do not know the name in Korean.

1. Where is the hotel?
1. The hotel is on the right side of the bakery. 2. It is across the one-way street from the electronics store. 3. It is across the street and south of the electronics store. 4. It is just north of the nightclub. It is above the nightclub. 5. It is across the street from the bookstore, on the west side of the main drag. 6. It is on the northeast corner (the top right corner) of the middle block.
2. Where is the health food store?
3. Where is the coffee shop?
4. How do you get from Popeye's to the gas station?
First, you go east, or to the right for one block. Then turn left at the nightclub and go north for one block. Next, turn right at the bookstore and go east for one block. Finally, it will be on the right side of the block, across the street from the handicapped parking.
5. How do you get from the 3-Story Villas to the cash machine?
6. How do you get to the post office from the health club?

11 DESCRIBING

 1 mustache

 2 balding, goatee

 3 bald, beard

 4 military cut

 5 shaved head

 6 shoulder-length, wavy, streaked hair

 7 bangs and short, thin, straight hair

 8 long, thick, wavy hair

 9 frizzy hair

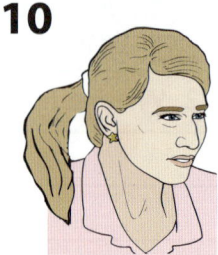 10 ponytail

1. He has straight hair, combed back and parted on the left. He is grinning, he has thick eyebrows, and he has a mustache. He is facing the right. He is wearing a coat and tie.
2. He is balding, and he has a goatee. He has wrinkles on his forehead and around his eyes. He is wearing a crewneck sweater.
3. He is bald, with black hair and a black beard. He is facing the right and smiling. He looks plump or even fat.
4. He has a dark complexion and a military haircut. He is wearing a V-neck shirt and he looks muscular.
5. He has a shaved head and a dark complexion. He's wearing a collared shirt, buttoned at the neck, but no tie.
6. She has shoulder-length, streaked hair that is parted slightly on the left. She is facing the left, and she has a serious expression.
7. She has short, thin, straight, light-colored hair and bangs. Her body is facing right, and her head is facing forward. She is wearing a collarless top.
8. She has long, thick, wavy dark-brown hair. She is facing the left, and she has long eyebrows. She has a mole on her cheek.
9. She has very thick, very frizzy long hair. She is smiling, and her face is kind of square. She has on big earrings and a low-cut V-neck top.
10. She has her long hair pulled back into a ponytail. She has a serious expression, and she is looking to the right. She has on a light-colored, collared top.

RECEDING HAIRLINE: Nicholas Cage, Tom Hanks
BALDING: Sean Connery, Gene Hackman, Bruce Willis
SALT & PEPPER (gray & black) **HAIR:** Richard Gere
STRONG JAW: Jay Leno
SQUARE FACE: Arnold Schwarzenegger
DIMPLES: Tom Cruise

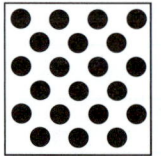 polka dot

 checkered

 thin vertical stripes

 thick horizontal stripes

 diagonal stripes

 plaid

 paisley

 50

1. She has long, thin, straight hair and bangs. She is wearing a sheer (see-through) top over a white body stocking. She is wearing tight dress jeans and calf-length, soft leather boots.

2. She also has long, thin hair with bangs, but her hair is a little wavy. She's wearing jewelry: earrings, a necklace, and a white bracelet. She's wearing a loose-fitting, peasant-type top, which has elbow-length sleeves and is gathered at the waist. She has a diagonal-striped short skirt and sandal-type high heels with straps.

3. She has long, thick, jet-black hair, but not bangs. She's wearing a light open-neck sweater. She has a bare midriff, barely. She's wearing camouflage cargo pants and flat sandals.

4. She has thick, black hair that is parted on the left and gathered in back. She's wearing a long-sleeved top and tight, boot-cut dress jeans. (Boot-cut means the bottoms are flared out to fit over boots. Jeans usually come in straight-leg, boot-cut, flared, and bell bottoms.) You can't see it, but her shoes are pumps, which means they are in between flats and high heels.

5. She's wearing a horizontal-striped, loose-fitting top with big, baggy short sleeves. She's wearing tight, calf-length blue jeans, and spiked high heels. (If her heels were a bit longer, they would be stiletto heels.)

6. She has thick black hair pulled back into a ponytail. She's wearing a low-cut sleeveless top, a knee-length print skirt, and sandals.

7. She has shoulder-length, thick brown hair and bangs. She's wearing a white leather jacket over a diagonal-striped top. She has on a blue jean mini-skirt, and she's wearing open-toed, medium-heeled shoes.

8. She has short, wavy hair. She's wearing a loose-fitting, short-sleeved top, a casual blue jean mini-skirt, and tennis shoes.

FEMALES

← FACING THE LEFT FACING THE RIGHT →

Descriptions p. 94

PLAN A:

1. Sit in a group of 3: A, B, and C.
2. A will secretly select a female and describe her.
   (A will be sneaky and hide her eyes, so that B and C cannot see where A is looking.)
3. B and C will guess who she is describing.
4. If B and C guess wrong, then they will ask questions to try to figure out who A is describing. They can use the questions below.
5. After they correctly guess A's model, it is B's turn. Then C's. Then A's again.
   Note: You could describe the person fully, and they could quickly guess the answer.
   Or you could give just a little information, to make them ask plenty of questions.

Example:

A   She has shoulder-length, slightly wavy hair.
B   Number 4! I win, I win!
A   Wrong.
C   Number 2! Number 2!
A   Wrong.
B   What color is her hair?
A   She has light hair.
C   Does she have bangs? Maybe number 23?
A   No.
B   Is she smiling?
A   No.
C   Is she happy or sad, young or old?
A   She is not smiling, but she doesn't look sad. She looks about 30.
B   Is her head leaning down toward the left, like number 32?
A   No.
C   What is she wearing?
A   She has on a striped top with no collar.
B   Are they horizontal or vertical stripes?
A   Horizonal stripes.
C   Number 12! Number 12!
A   Du-uh! Those are vertical stripes. Relax. Breathe deeply.
B   Which way is she facing?
A   She's facing left.
B   Number 14!
A   FINALLY! Right.

HELPFUL QUESTIONS
Is she average, pretty, or beautiful?
Is her hair long or short? Straight or wavy?
Is her hair light or dark? Thick or thin?
Does she have bangs? Are they straight?
Is her hair pulled back or parted?
Which side is it parted on?
Does she have a high hairline?
Does she have a strong or weak jaw?
Which way is she facing?
Are her clothes dressy or casual?
Is she smiling or serious?
Is her hair wild or combed?
Is her top a turtleneck or low-cut?
Is she wearing any jewelry?

PLAN B:

Same as method 1, except that A does NOT describe her selection. B and C begin by asking questions, and A answers only with a YES or NO, or only one word.

Example:

B   Is she young or old?
A   Young.
C   Does she have black hair?
A   No.
B   Does she have long hair?
A   No.
C   Does she have bangs?
A   Yes.
B   Is her hair straight or wavy?
C   Curly.

(And so on.)

PLAN C:
Describe your favorite female movie stars, foreign or Korean. Your partners will ask questions and try to guess.

You can describe their looks, build, personality, the kind of movies they make, and the kind of characters they usually play.

Hey! You can do the same with your favorite singer.

MALES

← PARTED ON THE RIGHT   PARTED ON THE LEFT →

Descriptions p. 95

PLAN A:
Same as Plan A for the females.

Example:

- A He has short, thin hair and he is middle-aged or a little older.
- B Is he wearing a coat and tie?
- A No.
- C Is he wearing a coat?
- A No.
- B Is he wearing sunglasses?
- A No.
- C Does he have a mustache or a beard?
- A No.
- B Is he bald, or does he have a receding hairline?
- A Well, maybe not a receding hairline, but at least he has a high forehead.
- C Number 8!
- A No, his hair is not exactly thin.
- B Is he facing to the right or the left?
- A He is looking straight ahead.
- C Does he have a Chinese collar shirt? Number 30!
- A Wrong.
- C Is he wearing a sweater?
- A Yes.
- B Is it a solid color or does it have a polka dot or diamond-pattern design?
- A Solid color.
- B Number 12!
- A No. But close.
- C Wait, wait. Number 34 is the same as 12, except that their hair is parted on different sides. Is it number 34?
- A BINGO!

HELPFUL QUESTIONS
Is his hair long or short? Thick or thin?
Is his hair straight or wavy? Light or dark?
Is he going bald and trying to hide it?
Is his hair combed back or parted on the side?
Which side is his hair parted on?
Is he smiling or frowning?
Is he happy or serious?
Is he wearing a coat? Light or dark?
Is he wearing a tie?
Is he looking straight ahead or to the side?
Does he have a beard or mustache?
Is he dressed up or casual?
Can you see his teeth?
About how old is he?

PLAN B:
Same as method 1, except that A does NOT describe his/her selection. B and C begin by asking questions, and A answers only with a YES or NO, or only one word.

Example:

- B Is he young or old?
- A Young.
- C Is he smiling?
- A Yes.
- B Can you see his teeth?
- A No.
- C Does he have bangs?
- A Yes.
- B Are his eyebrows thick or average?
- C Thick.

(And so on.)

PLAN C:
Describe your favorite male movie stars, foreign or Korean. Your partners will ask questions and try to guess.

You can describe their looks, build, personality, the kind of movies they make, and the kind of characters they usually play.

Try it with your favorite male singer also.

DESCRIPTIONS: FEMALES

1. She has long, wavy blond hair, which is parted on the left. She is smiling and her body is slightly facing the left. She is wearing a collarless top.
2. She has shoulder-length, dark brown hair, and she is facing the right. She is smiling slightly and she is wearing a horizontal-striped top.
3. She has long, thick, wavy black hair that is pulled back out of her face. She has long eyebrows and a strong jaw. Her dark top has no collar.
4. She has long, thick, wild, uncombed hair, and bangs. She is smiling and she has a thick lips, a big mouth, and big teeth. She is wearing a V-neck top.
5. She has neck-length thick, wavy dark hair. She is smiling and looking slightly down. She is wearing a low-cut, sleeveless top. It looks like it could be an aerobics outfit.
6. She has long, wavy black hair that falls in front of her shoulders. She has dark eye makeup and she is facing the right.
7. She has long hair that she is wearing up. She has a serious expression, and she has on a V-neck top.
8. She has long, very thick, frizzy hair. She is smiling and wearing earrings. She has on a low-cut top.
9. She has short, straight dark hair that is parted on the left. She has high cheekbones and is wearing a black blouse or jacket.
10. She has short, thin, straight hair that is combed forward. She is smiling broadly and she is facing the left. She has big eyes and a big mouth. Her shirt has a really big collar.
11. She has short hair that is combed in a man's hairstyle. She has a serious expression, and she has a V-neck top.
12. Same as number 2, but with vertical stripes and blonde hair.
13. She has long, thick, wavy black hair that is pulled back from her face. She has long eyebrows and a strong jaw. She has a high forehead and her dark top has no collar.
14. Same as number 2, but with light hair and facing the left.
15. Same as number 4, but with no makeup on. Or maybe she has acne.
16. She has long, very thick, frizzy hair. She has a serious expression, and her head is leaning a little down and toward the left. Her top has no collar.
17. She has short, straight, dark hair that is combed forward. Maybe she is wearing heavy eye makeup. She is looking straight ahead.
18. She has long, thick, wavy blond hair. She is facing right. She is wearing a bikini top, or a spaghetti strap, very low-cut dress. It's called a spaghetti strap because it is very thin, like a strand of spaghetti. Her top shows cleavage.
19. She has short, curly blond hair. She has a serious expression and she is facing the right. Her top is collarless.
20. She has short, thick hair with heavy bangs. Her hair is thicker on top than it is on the sides. She is smiling and looking straight ahead. She is wearing a turtleneck top.
21. She has short dark hair that is combed forward. She has bangs, big eyes, and a strong jaw. She's wearing earrings and a collared top. She is facing the left.
22. She has short curly hair, with a longer lock of hair behind each ear. Those are called ringlets. She's not smiling or frowning and she is facing the front. Her top has no collar.
23. She looks positively perky! She has shoulder-length hair that curls out at the shoulders. She has even bangs. She has a big smile and is facing the right.
24. Same as number 2, but with light hair.
25. Same as number 1, but her hair is parted on the right, and her body is facing right.
26. She has a "pageboy" hairdo: short, shoulder-length hair that curls in at the shoulders, and bangs. She is facing directly forward and wearing a turtleneck top.
27. Same as number 8, but with a turtleneck top.
28. She has long blond hair that is brushed back out of her face. She is facing straight ahead and wearing a T-shirt.
29. She has long, thick, dark hair that is brushed back. She has a strong jaw and long eyebrows. She has a low hairline and she is facing the left.
30. The same as number 18, but she is facing left and has a blue and white geometric pattern top.
31. She has dark, shoulder-length hair and maybe a perm. She has a big smile and is wearing a T-shirt.
32. She has shoulder-length thick black hair with bangs. She has long eyebrows. She is facing the left and her head is tilted slightly down. She's smiling.
33. Same as number 6, but with a dark complexion.
34. She has an angular face and has shoulder-length, very wavy hair—not quite curly, but close. She has big earrings, and she is wearing a strapless dress.
35. Same as number 2, but with vertical stripes and facing left.

DESCRIPTIONS: MALES

1. He looks like an aging rock star. He has short, thick hair with bangs. His hair is longer in the back than in the front. He's wearing sunglasses, a horizontal striped T-shirt, and a dark jacket.
2. He looks like a light-skinned African American. He has short curly hair and a goatee. He is facing the left and his head is tilted slightly down. He has a high forehead and he's wearing a bowtie.
3. He has short, curly dark hair and a receding hairline. He is facing straight ahead. He is smiling and wearing a T-shirt.
4. He looks like an accountant. He has short, straight, thin hair that is parted on the left. He has a collared shirt under a crew-neck, diamond-patterned sweater. He's wearing thin-framed glasses.
5. He has long, wavy light-colored hair. He has a mustache and an intense expression on his face. He is facing the left, and he's wearing a light, colored T-shirt and a dark coat.
6. Same as number 5, but a with dark hair and a light coat.
7. He is kind of old, and he looks plump or even pudgy. He is bald with gray hair and a goatee. He's trying to smile and he's wearing a blue, casual, collared shirt. dark T-shirt.
8. He's 30 to 40 and has a big smile. He has short, dark hair that is combed back. His hair is thicker on top than it is on the sides. He's wearing a casual, collared shirt.
9. He has short, brown, slicked-backed hair. (If hair has gel or mousse in it, it is called slicked.) He's facing the left, but he's looking this way. He has long, thick eyebrows. He's wearing a suit, a coat, and tie.
10. He's an African American. Same as number 2, but with a darker complexion.
11. Same as number 9 but facing the right.
12. Same as number 4, but his hair is parted on the right, and his sweater is a solid color.
13. Same as number 11, but with gray hair.
14. He is old, and his hair is kind of long for an old man. His hair is white and parted on the right. He's wearing rimmed glasses. He has on a white dress shirt and tie, and a vertical-striped sweater vest.
15. He's a little old and going bald, but he combs his hair forward to try to hide the baldness. His hair is thick on the sides, and he has sideburns. He has thick eyebrows and wrinkles around his eyes. He has on a casual shirt and a plaid coat.
16. The same as number 1, but with a solid-colored T-shirt and a dark jacket.
17. He's a little older, with short dark hair. His hair is graying at the temples. (Often, when men's hair turns gray, it starts at the temples.) He's wearing a coat and tie.
18. The same as number 4, but wearing a polka dot sweater.
19. Same as number 1, but with a light-colored coat.
20. He's wearing thick-rimmed glasses. He has short dark hair. He's wearing an open-collared shirt and coat.
21. Same as number 6 but facing the right.
22. He's an African American with thick, very curly hair. If his hairdo was a little thicker, you would call that an "Afro." He's wearing a suit and smiling broadly.
23. He has a high forehead and a receding hairline. He has short dark hair, long sideburns, and thick eyebrows. He's wearing a casual, collared shirt.
24. He is bald, with a beard, and he looks heavy. He's wearing a camouflaged sweater, and he has a little gap between his top front teeth.
25. Same as number 6, but he's facing right and has on a dark T-shirt.
26. Same as number 24, but facing the right.
27. Same as number 5, but facing the right, with a light-colored coat.
28. Same as number 1, but with a checkered T-shirt.
29. Same as number 15, but with a checkered jacket.
30. He has light-colored hair that is combed back. He's wearing a Chinese collar shirt.
31. Same as number 22, but his hair is close-cropped (shorter).
32. Same as number 1, but with a diagonal-striped T-shirt.
33. He has a high forehead and receding hairline. (Often, when a man's hairline starts to recede, he will let his hair grow longer in the back, to sort of compensate. The general rule is: As it gets thinner on top, it gets longer in the back.) His hair is thicker on the sides and thinner on top. He's smiling and wearing an open-collared casual shirt.
34. Same as number 12, but his hair is parted on the left.
35. He has a strong jaw. He has salt-and-pepper hair. (Salt is gray and pepper is black. So salt-and-pepper hair is black and gray hair.) He is arching his eyebrows.

12 CORE VOCABULARY

LOOKS, HAIR, & BUILD

 51

FEMALE LOOKS

ugly	못생긴
unattractive; homely	매력 없는
plain	평범한
so-so	그저 그런, 보통의
fair	보통의 외모인
average	보통의
OK	외모가 괜찮은
cute	귀여운, 예쁜
good-looking	잘생긴
pretty	예쁜
precious	가치 있는, 사랑스러운
beautiful	아름다운
gorgeous	매우 아름답고 멋진
stops traffic	매우 아름답고 근사한
drop-dead gorgeous	매우 멋지고 아름다운

MEN & WOMEN'S BUILD

(M = males only)

tall / short / medium	(키가) 큰, 작은, 중간인
thin / fat / average	날씬한 / 뚱뚱한 / 보통의
skin and bones	매우 마른
skinny	마른
slender	쭉 빠진
washboard stomach (M)	날씬한 배
muscular	근육질의
love handles (M)	아랫배의 군살
plump	통통한
pudgy	땅딸막한
stocky (M)	작고 단단한
heavy-set	체격 좋게 살찐
beer belly (M)	술배
obese	비만

WOMEN'S BUILD

voluptuous	가슴이 매우 큰 매력적인 몸매
hour-glass figure	허리가 잘록한 몸매
fine	멋진
long legs; legs up to here	긴 다리
plump	통통한
pleasingly plump	귀엽게 포동포동한

MALE LOOKS

ugly	못생긴
unattractive; homely	매력적이지 않은
plain	평범한
so-so	그저 그런, 보통의
fair	보통의 외모인
average	보통의
OK	괜찮은 외모의
cute	귀여운
good-looking	잘생긴
pretty boy	예쁘게 생긴 남자
ruggedly handsome	전체적으로 괜찮게 잘생긴
handsome	매우 잘생긴
(well-)built	몸짱

MEN'S HAIR

beard	턱수염
goatee	염소수염 (턱 밑)
mustache	콧수염 (Clark Gable)
sideburns	구레나룻 (Elvis)
hairy chest	가슴에 털이 있는
receding hairline	앞머리부터 빠져가는

WOMEN'S HAIR

bangs	짧게 자른 앞머리
colored; dyed	염색한
streaked	줄무늬 염색 (브릿지)
wavy	약간 부드럽게 곱슬거리는
curly	곱슬곱슬한
permed	파마한
frizzy	매우 곱슬거리는
pigtails	땋아 늘인 머리 (양쪽)
ponytail	한 가닥을 뒤로 묶은 머리
pulled back	뒤로 싹 넘겨 묶은 머리
parted in the middle	앞가르마의
in a bun	올린 머리

SKIN

silky-smooth	부드럽고 매끈한
like a baby's bottom	보드라운
soft, smooth	폭신한, 부드러운
milky-white	우유처럼 하얀
weathered	거칠고 햇볕에 탄
leathery	거친, 가죽처럼 질긴
acne; pitted; scarred	자국이 남은
wrinkled	주름진

CLOTHES

PANTS
baggy	헐렁한, 불룩한
straight leg	상하 넓이가 같은 일자 바지
boot-cut	아래통이 넓은 바지
flared	밑이 넓은 바지 / 스커트
bell-bottoms	나팔바지
shorts	반바지
cut-offs	무릎에서 자른 청바지
knee-length pants	무릎 길이의 바지
button-fly	지퍼 대신 단추로 된 바지

SKIRTS & DRESSES
pleated	주름진
ankle-length	발목까지 오는
calf-length	종아리까지 오는
knee-length	무릎까지 오는
miniskirt	미니스커트
wrap-around skirt	허리에 두르는 스커트
slit skirt	옆트임 치마
mini-dress	미니 드레스

TOPS
stripes: wide / thin	줄무늬: 넓은 것 / 가는 것
horizontal stripe	가로줄 무늬
vertical stripe	세로줄 무늬
bare midriff	배꼽티
checkered	체크무늬
flowered	꽃무늬
halter top	등이 많이 드러나는 옷
long-sleeved	긴 소매
low-cut	목이 깊게 파인 옷
print, pattern	그림이나 문양이 있는 옷
short-sleeved	짧은 소매
sleeveless	소매가 없는
spaghetti strap	가는 어깨끈으로 된 것
turtleneck	목을 감싸는 폴라
V-neck	목이 V모양으로 된 것
backless dress	등이 많이 파인 드레스
tank top	탱크톱
pajamas (PJ's)	파자마 (원피스 잠옷)
pantyhose	팬티스타킹
scarf	스카프
slip / full slip	슬립 / 속치마
stockings	스타킹
lingerie	디자인을 강조한 여성용 잠옷
underwear; undergarments	속옷
panties (for women)	여성팬티
one-piece swimsuit	(원피스) 수영복
bikini; two-piece	비키니
stained	얼룩진, 더러운 것이 묻은
ripped; torn	부분적으로 찢어진
shrink; shrunk	(잘못 세탁해서) 줄어든
pre-shrunk	줄어드는 것을 방지한

"This is too . . ."
tight	몸에 꽉 끼는
loose	느슨한, 성긴
light	밝은
dark	어두운, 칙칙한
bright	(빛깔이) 선명한, 산뜻한
loud	요란한 (빛깔)
thick	두꺼운
thin	얇은
sheer	얇은, 비치는
risqué; sexy	섹시한; 야한
out of style	유행에 뒤져있는
old-fashioned	구식의, 유행에 뒤져있는
tacky	초라한, 볼품없는

"This material is kind of . . ."
soft	부드러운, 매끈매끈한
hard	딱딱한, 견고한, 튼튼한
rough	거칠한, (털이) 헝클어진
smooth	매끄러운
wrinkled	주름진
wet	젖은, 축축한
dirty	지저분한
filthy	더러운, 불결한
smelly	(고약한) 냄새나는

MATERIAL
fur / fake fur	모피 / 인조가죽
leather	가죽
polyester	폴리에스터
polyester blend	폴리에스터 합성섬유
cotton 면	silk 비단
velvet 우단	wool 모

MEN'S STUFF
button-down collar	셔츠깃 끝을 단추로 고정
dress shirt	정장 셔츠
polo shirt	스포츠 셔츠
muscle shirt	소매가 없는 셔츠
jersey	운동선수복의 상의 (축구, 럭비)
suspenders	멜빵
belt	벨트
cargo pants	주머니가 많은 작업용 바지
permanent press	구김을 방지하는 영구가공
wrinkle-free	구김이 잘 생기지 않는

SUITS
two- / three-button	단추가 2개 / 3개 있는 양복 상의
single-breasted	양복 상의가 겹치지 않게 입는
double-breasted	양복 상의가 겹치게 입는
blazer	단체복 상의의 일종

COATS
bomber jacket	항공 점퍼, 군용 재킷
trench coat	트렌치 코트 (바바리)
windbreaker	방한, 방풍용의 스포츠재킷

SHOES
tennis	테니스화
dress	정장화
jogging	조깅화
platform	굽이 두꺼운 캐주얼화

FOOTWEAR
pumps	굽이 약간 있는 신발	high heels	하이힐
		flats	굽이 낮은 신발
sandals	샌달		
hiking boots	등산화	slippers	슬리퍼

ACCESSORIES
bracelet	팔찌	necklace	목걸이
brooch	브로치	purse	여성지갑
handbag	핸드백	wallet	남성지갑

JOBS

1	accountant	회계사
2	actor / actress	남자배우 / 여배우
3	anchorman / anchorwoman	남자앵커 / 여자앵커
4	artist	예술가
5	attorney	변호사
6	banker	은행원
7	bartender	바텐더
8	businessman	벽돌공
9	CEO	사업가
10	chauffeur	자가용 운전사
11	chef	최고경영자
12	clerk: bank / post office	사무원(은행, 우체국)
13	computer graphics designer	컴퓨터 그래픽 디자이너
14	computer programmer	컴퓨터 프로그래머
15	construction worker	공사장 인부
16	dancer	무용가, 댄서
17	dentist	치과의사
18	detective	형사
19	diplomat	외교관
20	director / producer	감독 / 제작자
21	doctor	의사
22	electrician	전기공
23	engineer	기술자
24	entrepreneur	사업가
25	farmer	농부
26	firefighter	소방관
27	hairstylist	미용사
28	interior decorator	실내장식가
29	interpreter	통역사
30	journalist	신문잡지 기자
31	judge	판사
32	lawyer	변호사
33	librarian	사서
34	mailman	집배원
35	military officer / soldier	군인
36	minister; pastor	성직자, 외교관, 장관, 목사
37	monk	승려, 수사
38	nurse	간호사
39	pilot	조종사
40	plumber	배관공
41	politician	정치가
42	priest	카톨릭 신부
43	reporter	리포터
44	salesclerk	판매원
45	salesperson	판매원
46	scientist	과학자
47	secretary	비서
48	self-employed	자영업의
49	stewardess; flight attendant	여자 승무원, 남자 승무원
50	surgeon	외과의사
51	tailor	재단사
52	truck driver	트럭 운전사
53	**blue-collar worker**	노무직 종사자
54	**white-collar worker**	사무직 종사자

MAJORS

Accounting	회계학
Advertising	광고학
Agriculture	농학
Agronomy	농업경제학
Architecture	건축학
Art	예술전공
Art History	예술사
Biology	생물학
Business Administration	경영학
Chemical Engineering	화학공학
Chemistry	화학
Chinese	중국어
Computer Graphics	컴퓨터그래픽
Dance	무용
Drama	연극영화
Economics	경제학
Electrical Engineering	전기공학
Engineering	공학, 기관학
Environmental Science	환경과학
Fashion Design	의상디자인
Fine Arts	순수미술
Food & Nutrition	식품 경영학
General Business	일반 경영학
Geography	지질학
Health Science	보건학
Herbal (Chinese) Medicine	한의학
History	역사
Info. & Comm. Technology	정보통신기술학
Interior Design	실내장식
Japanese	일본어
Law	법학
Library & Information Science	문헌정보학
Life Science	생명과학
Mathematics	수학
Mechanical Engineering	기계공학
Medicine	의학도(의과대생)
Music	음악
Natural Science	자연과학
Nursing	간호학
Pharmacy	약학
Philosophy	철학
Physics	물리학
Psychology	심리학
Public Administration	행정학
Radio & TV Broadcasting	방송학
Safety Engineering	안전공학
Theology	신학
Tourism	관광학과
Urban Planning	도시계획
Zoology	동물학
graduate school	대학원
humanities	인문학부
social sciences	사회학부
liberal arts	교양학부

PERSONALITY ACRONYMS

1	absent-minded	건망증이 있는
2	adorable	존경할 만한, 사랑스러운
3	ambitious	야망 있는
4	artistic	미적 감각이 있는
5	blunt	무딘, 무뚝뚝한
6	bossy	남을 다스리고자 하는
7	charismatic	카리스마적인
8	clever	영리한
9	closed- / open-minded	옹졸한 / 편견 없는
10	compassionate	동정을 많이 주는
11	conformist	반항적인 사람
12	conservative	보수주의자
13	considerate	사려 깊은
14	cooperative	협동적인
15	creative	창조적인
16	creepy	소름끼치는
17	demure	차분한, 얌전한
18	diplomatic	외교적인
19	disgusting	구역질 나는, 꼴불견의
20	easygoing	편안한 성격의
21	gracious	자비로운, 인자한
22	gregarious	사교적인
23	grouchy	토라진
24	hyper	몹시 흥분한
25	immature	미숙한
26	impulsive	충동적인
27	insecure	믿을 수 없는
28	intellectual	지적인
29	intolerant	완고한
30	irresponsible	무책임한
31	laid-back	느긋한
32	loyal	충실한
33	mean	비열한, 못된
34	mellow	원만한
35	mild-mannered	온순한
36	mischievous	장난을 좋아하는
37	moody	우울한
38	narrow-minded	마음이 좁은
39	nonconformist	관행을 따르지 않는 사람
40	obnoxious	역겨운
41	optimistic	낙천주의의
42	passionate	열정적인
44	pessimistic	비관적인
45	secretive	비밀스런
46	self-confident	자신만만한
47	selfish	이기적인
48	sensitive	섬세한
49	spoiled	버릇없는
50	stubborn	완고한
51	sweet	상냥한
52	temperamental	변덕스러운
53	tolerant	인내심이 강한
54	troublemaker	문제아, 말썽꾸러기
55	well-informed	박식한

Acronym	Meaning
AKA	also known as
ASAP	as soon as possible
BYOB	bring your own beer
CEO	chief executive officer
CIA	Central Intelligence Agency
DUI	driving under the influence
DWI	driving while intoxicated
FBI	Federal Bureau of Investigation
FDA	Food & Drug Administration
FYI	for your information
GPA	grade point average
ID	identification
IOU	"I owe you" (a debt)
IRS	Internal Revenue Service
MBA	Master's of Business Administration
MLB	Major League Baseball
NATO	North Atlantic Treaty Organization
P.S.	postscript
RSVP	*Respondez s'il vous plait.* (Please respond to the invitation.)
SOS	save our ship (a call for help)
TGIF	thank goodness it's Friday
UFO	unidentified flying object
UN	United Nations
VIP	very important person

EDUCATION

GMAT	Graduate Management Admission Test
GRE	Graduate Record Exam
LSAT	Law School Admission Test
TOEIC	Test of English for International Communication
TOEFL	Test of English as a Foreign Language

DEGREES

BA / BS	Bachelor of Arts / Science
MA / MS	Master of Arts / Science
ABD	all but dissertation (almost a PhD)
PhD	doctor of philosophy

MILITARY

AWOL	absent without leave
MIA / KIA	missing in action / killed in action
POW	prisoner of war

CHATTING

BFF	best friends forever
BRB	be right back
JK	just kidding
LOL	laughing out loud
NP	no problem
OMG	oh my gosh!
RT	retweet
SMH	shaking my head
TMI	too much information
TTYL	talk to you later
YOLO	you only live once

13 CORE SKILLS

 57

HOW OFTEN?
all the time
always
almost always
as often as possible
every chance I get
most of the time
frequently
often
regularly
usually
generally
normally
sometimes
occasionally
on occasion
every now and then
on special occasions
not too often
seldom
rarely
very seldom
hardly ever
once in a blue moon
never
never ever
when pigs fly

FREQUENCY
once a day / week / month / year
twice a day / week / month / year
three times a day / week / month / year
four times a day / week / month / year
every other day / week / month / year

PASSAGE OF TIME
ten years / months / days ago
the day before yesterday
last night
this morning
today
this afternoon
this evening
tonight
tomorrow
tomorrow morning / afternoon / night
the day after tomorrow
next week / month / year
in two days / weeks / months / years

QUALITY
awesome
magnificent
fantastic
superb
wonderful
fabulous
excellent
outstanding
very good
great
pretty good
good
OK; fair; so-so
mediocre
It will do.
no smash hit
You didn't miss a thing.
poor
bad
pretty bad
lame
awful
terrible
horrible
the pits
It stank.

LIKES TO DISLIKES

1. I adore Brad Pitt.
2. I really love to travel.
3. I love going to nightclubs.
4. I enjoy cooking.
5. I like shopping in Apkujong.
6. I don't mind taking the bus.
7. I don't care for diet cola.
8. I don't like to study all night.
9. I really don't like to wake up early.
10. I hate rude people.
11. I can't stand people who lie.
12. I detest arrogant people.

BODY PARTS

hair	머리카락	cheeks	볼	shoulder	어깨	throat	목구멍	bladder	방광
scalp	두피	dimples	보조개	armpit	겨드랑이	chest	흉부	buttocks	궁둥이의
skin	피부	mouth	입	arm	팔	heart	심장	butt	엉덩이
brain	뇌	tooth / teeth	치아	elbow	팔꿈치	lungs	폐	thigh	허벅다리
forehead	이마	gums	잇몸	forearm	팔뚝	ribs	늑골	knee	무릎
eyebrows	눈썹	tongue	혀	wrist	손목	stomach	위	calf	종아리
eyelashes	속눈썹	tonsils	편도선	palm	손바닥	liver	간장	shin	정강이
eyes	눈	chin	턱끝	thumb	엄지	kidney	신장	ankle	발목
nose	코	jaw	아래턱	finger	손가락	intestines	장	foot / feet	발
nostrils	콧구멍	neck	목	knuckle	손가락 마디	waist	허리	toes	발가락

FREQUENCY

Knowing how to talk about frequency is very important. It indicates your English skill level. For example, an English interview might begin with an easy question: "Do you have a hobby?" If you answer, "Yes, I play the piano," then you might be asked, "How often do you play the piano?" Your English level can then be determined by how you answer.

"Three times a week" indicates good English skill.
"Three a week" indicates a lower level of skill.

To be precise and clear when answering a frequency question, especially to someone of another culture, you should never answer with just "often" or "frequently." How often is "often"?

One person's "often" might be **once a week**, and another's might be **once a month**. Therefore, when answering a "how often" question, answer it using two expressions of frequency.
For example:

> How often do you see your grandmother? **Pretty often**, about **once a week**.
> I go to the movies **every now and then**, about **once every two months**.
> We get Chinese food delivered **very seldom**, maybe **once every three months**.
> I go to a coffee shop **as often as possible**, about **four times a week**.
> I exercise **once in blue moon**. Maybe **once a year**.
> I **seldom** drink, maybe about **three times a year**.

Note: **usually**, **generally**, and **normally** are used interchangeably. For example,
I **usually** wake up at 10. I **generally** wake up at 10. I **normally** wake up at 10.

QUALITY

You could probably describe quality with only these expressions: **good**, **bad**, **very**, and **so-so**.
My vacation was **very good** / **good** / **so-so** / **bad** / **very bad**.
This would mean that your English is so-so. So let's fix that.
The previous page contains twenty-six words to express that something was good or bad. The words go from **best** at the top, to **worst** at the bottom. A few of the expressions require their own structure, so here are some examples.

> My blind date was **awesome**.
> My vacation was **magnificent** / **fantastic** / **superb** / **wonderful** / **fabulous** / **excellent** / **outstanding** / **very good** / **great** / **pretty good** / **OK** / **fair** / **so-so** / **mediocre**.
> How was the new restaurant?
> **It will do**. **It was no smash hit**. It was **poor** / **bad** / **pretty bad** / **lame** / **awful** / **terrible** / **horrible**.
> How was the party?
> **It was the pits**.
> **It stank**.

TIME

THIS WEEKEND, NEXT WEEKEND:

On Monday, Tuesday, or Wednesday, if you say, "Next weekend, I will visit my hometown," you mean the coming weekend, a few days later.

But on Thursday or Friday, if you say, "Next weekend, I will visit my hometown," you mean the following weekend, eight or nine days later.

COMPARISON HELP

Rule 1 One-syllable words, such as big, tall, fast, smart
My car is bigger than yours.
My father is taller than yours.
My computer is faster than yours.
My dog is smarter than yours.

Rule 2 Two-syllable words that end in "y," such as pretty, dirty, curly, funny
My sister is prettier than yours.
Your blue jeans are dirtier than mine.
My hair is curlier than yours.
Dumb and Dumber was funnier than *Charlie's Angels*.

Rule 3 Two-syllable words, such as handsome, polite, clever, selfish
My boyfriend is more handsome than yours.
My mother is more polite than yours.
My brother is more clever than yours.
Your sister is more selfish than mine.

Rule 4 Three (or more)-syllable words, such as beautiful, intelligent, horrible, traditional
My dress is more beautiful than yours.
My pure breed dog is more intelligent than your mutt.
My blind date was more horrible than yours.
My grandfather is more traditional than yours.

Here, try a few.

My boyfriend
My favorite singer
My cell phone
My winter coat
My computer
My class schedule
My bedroom

 58

SOME COMMON OPPOSITES

큰	big	small	작은	좋은	good	bad	나쁜	똑똑한	smart	dumb	멍청한
밝은	bright	dim	흐릿한	우아한	graceful	awkward	서투른	매끄러운	smooth	rough	거친
깨끗한	clean	dirty	더러운	높은	high	low	낮은	부드러운	soft	hard	딱딱한
깊은	deep	shallow	얕은	뜨거운	hot	cold	차가운	자극적인	spicy	bland	자극 없는
쉬운	easy	difficult	어려운	밝은	light	dark	어두운	강한	strong	weak	약한
먼	far	near	가까이	정돈된	neat	dirty	지저분한	키가 큰	tall	short	키가 작은
빠른	fast	slow	느린	예의 바른	polite	rude	버릇 없는	두꺼운	thick	thin	얇은
뚱뚱한	fat	skinny	깡마른	부유한	rich	poor	가난한	넓은	wide	narrow	좁은
평평한	flat	bumpy	울퉁불퉁한	날카로운	sharp	dull	무딘	어린, 젊은	young	old	나이 든, 늙은

14 EXPLANATIONS & EXAMPLES

Unit 1	ALL ABOUT ME	104
Unit 2	WEEKENDS & NEIGHBORHOODS	108
Unit 3	TECHNOLOGY	111
Unit 4	DATING & NIGHTLIFE	112
Unit 5	SOFA TIME	118
Unit 6	HEALTH & FITNESS	119
Unit 7	HOLIDAYS & FESTIVALS	122
Unit 8	WORKING & GETTING THERE	124

1 ALL ABOUT ME

big spender: someone who spends a lot of money and buys expensive things. A big spender can be genuinely rich, or can spend more money than they can afford.
My uncle is a big spender. He always pays whenever the whole family goes out to eat.
My aunt is a big spender. She has an expensive car, expensive clothes, and expensive jewelry.

cheap: not liking to spend money
He is very cheap. He would rather walk two miles than take a taxi.
My husband is too cheap. For our anniversary, he took me out to eat at Burger King.

cheapskate: someone who does not like to spend money (less polite than calling someone "cheap")
That man's a cheapskate. He never leaves a tip

tightwad: someone who does not like to spend money. (a little more polite than calling someone a "cheapskate")
What a cheapskate. = What a tightwad.
Don't be such a cheapskate. = Don't be such a tightwad.

clean freak, neat freak: an excessively clean person
My mother is a neat freak. She cleans the house twice a day.
I'm not a clean freak, but I like things to be tidy.
My mother is such a neat freak that she irons my father's underwear and socks.

tidy: very neat and orderly. If someone says, "I am not a clean freak, but I like things tidy," they are a clean freak.
If someone is really excessive about being a clean freak, they might have an obsessive-compulsive disorder.

slob: a very messy person
My brother is a slob. There are things growing in his room.
I liked Jack until I went to his apartment. He's a slob.

couch potato: someone who sits on a sofa all day, reading or watching TV
What did you do last weekend? Nothing. I was a couch potato. I watched TV from Friday night to Sunday morning.
Stop being a couch potato and come to the movies with us.

active: energetic, always doing something
You are always so active—where do you get your energy?
My mother is very active in her church. She plays the piano and teaches Bible school every Sunday.

always on the go: active, always doing something, always in motion
Jill is always on the go. She's either shopping, or playing tennis, or helping at church, or cleaning her house. I get tired just talking to her.
Since I got promoted from technician to sales, I'm always on the go.

early bird: a person who gets up early
My father is an early bird. He's up at 5 every morning and jogs three miles before my mom wakes up.

The early bird catches the worm: a common saying that means that good things happen to people who get started early

night owl: someone who stays up very late—similar to an evening person, but much later
My sister is a night owl. She stays up until about 4 am every night.
On the weekends, she's a night owl. The sun is up before she gets home.

introvert: someone who tends to be thoughtful and quiet, and who gets tired from too much socializing
I'm an introvert, so I don't like making small talk with strangers.
My girlfriend's a shy introvert, but I'm pretty outgoing.

extravert: someone who tends to be outgoing and talkative, and who gets energy from socializing
Sales is a good career for an extravert.
She's such an extravert. She makes friends with everyone she meets.

generous, unselfish, giving: willing to give help, time, money, etc. to other people
My boss is very generous. = My boss is a very generous person.
My brother is generous with his time and talents. He coaches Little League baseball for free.

stingy: wanting all or most of something, while others have little or nothing. If you win a million dollars in the lottery and you give your unemployed brother ten dollars, you are stingy.
Don't be so stingy. Stop being stingy.
He had a hundred cookies, and he would not give you one? That is stingy.

selfish: thinking of yourself more than others; not generous
Stop being selfish and share your toys with your brother.

renege: to break a promise
Dan said he would give me his old phone, but then he reneged.

gourmet: someone who really likes and appreciates fine (and usually expensive) food
My brother is a gourmet. He spends a lot of time selecting ingredients and cooking, and he only eats at the finest restaurants.

foodie: someone who really loves food and knows a lot about it
Jen is a such a foodie. She's always eating out and talking about food.

food connoisseur: a fancy expression for "gourmet." A connoisseur has fine (and usually expensive) tastes. You could also be an art connoisseur or a wine connoisseur.
"Where will you take your brother to eat?" "That's a difficult choice. He's such a food connoisseur."

picky eater: someone who is very selective about the food they eat
My niece is a picky eater. She took everything green off her pizza before she ate it.
You're a picky eater. Can't you just order a regular hamburger like everybody else? You're taking forever to decide.

junkfood junkie: someone who loves junk food. Junk food is food that is bad for you, and often it is fast food. "Junkie"' is slang for "addict."
I'm a junk-food junkie. It seems everything I eat comes from Dunkin Donuts or Baskin Robbins.
I love junk food. It's fast and cheap and there are no dishes to wash.

chocoholic: someone who is addicted to chocolate
My sister is a chocoholic. She eats three candy bars a day.

have a sweet tooth: to really likes sweets: chocolates, pastry, candy, desserts
"Do you have a sweet tooth?" "Yes, but my dentist keeps telling me I have to stop eating so much sugar."
I don't drink, smoke, or gamble, but I have a sweet tooth. I love pastry and ice cream and candy.

eat anything: Some people are very picky, selective, and choosy about what they eat. They are hard to please. There is no idiom for the opposite of a picky eater. We just say that they eat anything. Everything tastes great.
"Are you a picky eater?" "No, I eat anything."

joiner: someone who joins many clubs and likes to belong to groups
I wasn't a joiner until I went to college. Now I belong to three clubs.
My younger sister is shy, but my older brother's a joiner.

loner: someone who likes, or does not mind, being alone. Very shy people and introverts are often loners.
My daughter was a loner in high school. I hope she makes some friends in college.
I've always been kind of a loner. Give me a good book and a soft sofa, and I am happy.

kind: very nice; generous
She found your wallet and brought it all the way to your house? That was very kind.
You are a kind person.

kind of: a little bit (often pronounced "kinda")
"Are you hungry?" "Kind of."
"How do you feel?" "Not too good. I got kind of drunk last night."

mean: unkind; cruel
Jack is a mean child. He makes fun of other kids.
He was nice until we broke up, and then he got very mean.
Why are you always so mean to your sister?

leader: someone who takes charge and decides what to do; someone other people want to follow
Jack is the leader of that group. They always do what he says.

follower: someone who goes along with the leader
I wish she were more of a leader, but she has always been a follower.
If you want to be rich, you can't be a follower. Most rich people are leaders.

long attention span; short attention span: If you have a long attention span, you can study or concentrate for a long time (three to four hours). If you have a short attention span, you can only study, or concentrate, for a short time (twenty to thirty minutes). Generally, children (especially boys) have short attention spans. They ask things like: "Are we there yet?"
I had a long attention span in high school, but these days I need to take a break every half hour and take a nap every two hours.
I have a short attention span. I can never study more than one hour without taking a break.

have patience: to be able to wait or endure without complaining (Do not confuse with hospital patients.)
My mother has a lot of patience, so she never gets upset.
I used to have patience, but the older I get, the less patience I have.
My patience is wearing thin. Stop that or else.

have a short fuse: to get angry very easily, very quickly
Our taxi driver had a short fuse. He blew the horn and yelled at every red light.
My professor is a nice guy, but he has a short fuse for cell phones going off in class.

messy, a mess: not neat or tidy, someone or something that is not neat or tidy. Their house, room, or desk is a little disorganized and/or dirty.
Is your room always this messy?
Is your homework always this messy?
Your room is a mess! Clean it up!

neat: clean and tidy; cool; good
How do you keep your desk so neat? Mine is a mess.(clean, tidy)
Hey, this new tablet is neat (cool; good).

modest: not very proud or confident; humble
Even though he's a big movie star, he's very modest and nice.
"My English isn't very good." "You're being too modest. You speak excellent English."

stuck-up; conceited; vain: having a too-high opinion of yourself
I don't like her. She's stuck-up.
He's so vain. He's always taking selfies.
I was conceited until I came in last in the beauty contest. That cured me.

morning person: someone who is at their best or most productive in the morning
In high school, I was a morning person because I had no choice. But now I sleep till noon every day.
I'm a morning person. I cannot study after 5 p.m.
My father's a morning person. He wakes up at 5 every day and plays badminton before breakfast.

evening person: someone who is most productive in the evening
I'm an evening person, so I don't come alive until after noon.
While in graduate school, I became an evening person. I'd study until 2 or 3 a.m. and sleep till noon.
I'm an evening person. I do my best studying after 9 or 10 p.m. I just can't concentrate in the morning.

outgoing: not shy; an extravert
Jill is so outgoing. She makes friends in minutes.
I was too shy in high school. I'm going to be more outgoing in college.

shy: reserved, quiet; an introvert
I was shy when I first got to college, but now that I've made new friends, it's cool.
Jack is shy until his third beer, and then he's an extravert.

overachiever; underachiever: An underachiever is a smart person who performs below their abilities or potential. If you are very smart but you getonly Cs, you are an underachiever. An overachiever is the opposite; this is someone who tries so hard that they have the best grades in class.
Look at this. He has the highest IQ in class and the lowest grades. What an underachiever. Time to talk to his parents.
I am worried that my son is an underachiever. He graduated from Seoul National University, but he's a taxi driver. I hope it's just a phase he's going through.
Sometimes, the overachievers try too hard and they end up quitting and dropping out.

party animal: someone who likes to stay out late and party
Bill was a party animal right after he got out of the army.
Wow! Jack is a party animal, but he is so shy at work.
Those engineering majors are a bunch of party animals. They study hard and drink hard.

party pooper: someone who wants to go home early from the party; someone who does not want to party ("Pooped" is slang for "tired.")
It's only 10 o'clock! Don't be such a party pooper.
My date was a party pooper. Just when things were getting started, she wanted me to take her home.

perky: happy and cheerful (usually describes a girl). Meg Ryan and Reese Witherspoon usually play perky characters.
"You're always so perky. How do you do it?" "That's my job. I'm a cheerleader."
"What happened? Did you forget to take your perky pill today?" "No, my boyfriend went into the army yesterday."

grouch: someone who is always in a bad mood
You're complaining about a C? Don't be such a grouch. You were lucky to get that.

grouchy: unhappy, in a bad mood
My sister is always grouchy when she wakes up before 8.
My husband is grouchy before his first cup of coffee.
Her baby is getting grouchy. It must be time for her nap.

cranky: unhappy, in a bad mood (Cranky is also used often with infants who are too young to speak. They cannot express what is wrong with them, so they just cry and yell to show their unhappiness.)
Oh, the baby is cranky. I should go check to see if her diaper is wet.

polite: having good manners
Jane is such a polite child.
It was very polite of you to give that pregnant lady a seat.

rude: Impolite, having bad manners
Being late is rude. Get to class on time.
Why were you rude to the waitress? It was not her fault.

punctual: on time
I am always punctual. I hate being late.
My professor is too punctual. His classes begin on time, and not one minute later.

late: not on time
If you are late one more time, we are through.
Being late is rude. Get here on time.

skeptical: not believing something easily. A skeptical person wants to see proof.
She said her dog ate her homework, but I'm skeptical.
She says she slept at a friend's house, but I'm skeptical.

gullible: believing just about anything
My sister is gullible. The used-car salesman told her that the car had been owned by a grandmother who only used it to go to church once a week. And she bought it!

strict (bad cop): harsh, severe (Professors sometimes have to be both good cop and bad cop [at different times, of course]) A teacher might be a bad cop (to scold a class after they do poorly on a test) and a good cop (to encourage them). A teacher can also play "good cop-bad cop" all in one scene!)
"You are late, you get an 'F'!" "Oh, professor, please!" "Well, OK. You can take a makeup test tomorrow."
Is your father the good cop or the bad cop?

lenient (good cop): permissive, easygoing In movies and TV, policemen and detectives usually have partners, and one partner is usually strict, mean, violent, and the other is non-violent, sympathetic, and helpful. Often, they are just pretending so that they can scare somebody into cooperating. (Parents might do this also). Instead of saying: My father is strict and my mother is lenient, you could say: My mom is the good cop and my dad is the bad cop.
Do your parents play 'good cop-bad cop' when you come home late?

technophile: a lover of technology (The ending –phile means "someone who likes/loves.")
My boss is a real technophile. He thinks that every problem can be solved by technology, so we have all the latest technology in our office.

techno-geek; techie: someone who loves technology and knows a lot about it (similar to technophile)
My brother is a techno-geek. He has all the new technology.

technophobic / technophobe: having a fear of new technology / someone who is technophobic (The ending -phobic means "afraid of.")

My mother is technophobic. She does not trust new technology. She still has her typewriter.
My mother is a technophobe. I bought her a digital camera, but she still uses her old film camera.

totally honest; honest to a fault: truthful, too honest. Perhaps you should tell a little lie rather than be so honest.
He's honest to a fault. He should lie or at least learn to be a little more diplomatic.

tell white lies: to tell innocent, harmless lies, often in orderto be polite
"How do you like my new hairdo?" "It's very attractive."
"Do you think I'll get into Harvard?" "Of course."
"How was my singing?" "Amazing!"(amazingly bad)

weekend warrior: a person who drinks very heavily, but only on the weekend. A typical weekend warrior might be a student or businessman who studies or works hard during the week, then drinks hard on Friday and Saturday night.
Bill's a weekend warrior—you should have seen him last night dancing on the bar.
I was a weekend warrior in college, but not these days.

social drinker: a person who drinks moderate amounts of alcohol for social reasons
In college, I was a weekend warrior, but these days I'm just a social drinker. I only drink at family and work events.

teetotaler: someone who never drinks
My mother is a teetotaler.
"How was your date?" "Kind of a waste of money. The party had free booze, but she was a teetotaler."

prepared; well-prepared: ready. These words describe somebody who plans ahead and does their work ahead of time. They do not wait until the last minute.
My science majors are always well-prepared. That makes them easy to teach.

good to go: ready to go
"Are you ready for the test?" "I'm good to go."
"Our plane leaves at four. Are you ready?" "I'm good to go."
"Your speech is next. Are you nervous?" "I'm good to go."

procrastinate: to put off, or to delay, something as long as possible; to be a procrastinator
"Have you selected a major yet?" "No, I'm still procrastinating. I like art, but there's no money in it."
"What are you doing?" "Procrastinating. I can't decide whether to study or clean my room."
"Are you a procrastinator like your sister?" "Yeah, it runs in the family."

2 WEEKENDS &NEIGHBORHOODS

Weekend Words

catch up on: to do things that you are behind on
I really need to catch up on my English homework. I'm way behind the other students.

fall behind: to not be up to date with work
I can't go out this weekend. I'm starting to fall behind in my classes.

hang out with (not play with): to spend free time with someone
I hung out with my boyfriend all weekend.

look forward to: to await something with excitement
I love giving and receiving presents. I always look forward to Christmas.

performance: a live entertainment event
Let's go to Hongdae to see her performance. It should be fun.

quality time: relaxing time when you can enjoy each other's company
My boss wanted me to work this weekend, but I told him I needed some quality time with my daughter.
I wish I could spend more quality time with my kids, but after work, I have to cook and clean.

rewarding: pleasing, satisfying
Volunteering is a very rewarding experience. I always feel great when I help others.

tentative plans: possible, usually hopeful plans, but not definite plans
I have tentative plans to visit my grandmother this weekend, but I may have to work.
We have tentative plans to go skiing this winter, but we have not been able to make reservations yet.

Relaxing Terms

chill, chill out: to relax
I had a very busy week. I'm just going to chill this weekend.

goof off: to waste time and do nothing productive
Don't goof off in class. The teacher is going to get angry at you.

kick back: to relax and take it easy
I love to kick back on Friday night and watch a movie. It is so relaxing.

R&R: rest and relaxation
My dad works so hard. I think he needs to get away for some R&R.

recharge my batteries: to relax and take it easy (another way of saying "rest and relax." At the end of the day, your cell phone battery needs to be recharged, and so do you.)
Last weekend, I just stayed home and recharged my batteries.

take it easy: to relax
"What did you do last weekend?" "Not much, I just stayed home and took it easy."

unwind: to relax after doing work or something else that is stressful
I've been staying late every night to finish the project. I really need to unwind this weekend.

Moody Terms

anxious: nervous, worried
I was anxious before I met his parents.
I was anxious when they wanted to talk to me at customs.

cranky, grouchy: irritable, in a bad mood
Bill is not a morning person. He is always cranky in the morning. It's not until after lunch that he stops being so grouchy.

depressed: very sad
I'm depressed. My boyfriend went into the army last month, my best friend went to Australia for the summer, and it's been raining all week.

drained: exhausted, mentally or physically; similar to "burnt out"
We played tennis for four hours in the hot sun. I'm drained.
I wrote that whole term paper in one night. I'm drained.

have (got) the blues: (slang) to be depressed
I've got the blues. My boyfriend went into the army.

pout: to be a little sad, but to pretend to be very sad
Stop pouting. I didn't yell at you. I was yelling at the computer.
No ice cream until you finish your homework. Now stop pouting and go do it.
Stop that or I'll give you something to pout about!

Tired Terms

burned out or **burnt out:** finished, all done; mentally exhausted after a long effort
I was burnt out after high school. I did not feel like studying in college until my junior year.
I'm taking a break this weekend. I worked seventy hours last week, and I am burnt out.

drained; exhausted: very tired mentally or physically or both
I'm exhausted. That was my last marathon.
That is the last time I babysit for twins. I'm exhausted.

sick and tired: angry about something that has happened repeatedly
I am sick and tired of you coming home late.
I am sick and tired of your filthy room.

stressed; stressed out: unhappy because of mental pressure
My job gives me stress. I'm stressed at work.
My job stresses me out. I'm stressed out at work.
I commute an hour and a half each way to work every day. But I don't mind, because by the time I get home I am no longer stressed out.

Sleeping Terms

catching some Z's: (slang) sleeping
"Where's Bill?" "He's on the sofa catching some Z's."

crash: (slang) to sleep
Jack and I went drinking, and I crashed at his house.
I'm tired. I'm going to crash.

dead to the world: in a very deep sleep
After studying for three midterm tests in one night, I went to bed and was dead to the world.

nap: sleep for a short time in the afternoon. Some naps are long, and some are short. If you are a businessperson and have a short but intense nap, and wake up ready and energized, it is called a "power nap."
"Do you take naps?" "I was napping when you called."
"Did you take a nap today?" "I must have. The dog chewed a hole in the sofa, and I never heard a thing."

play possum: to pretend to be asleep. This comes from the opossum, an animal that pretends to be dead as part of its defense against other animals.
Don't play possum with me. I know you're not asleep. Get up and clean your room.
My dad wanted me to help him clean the car, but I was playing possum.
Here are some advanced sleeping terms for you English ninja wannabes.

MORE SLEEPING TERMS

spaced out: almost asleep, have your brain wander (think of other things). The professor is lecturing, and Jack is thinking about a girl he met last night, and the professor says: *Jack, is that right?* Jack would say: *Oh, sorry professor, I spaced out for a second.*
"Did you take a nap?" "No, but I kind of spacedout for a couple of minutes."
I tried to pay attention, but I kept spacing out and thinking about my boyfriend cheating on me.

conked out: exhausted and sleeping. "Conked" means to be hit on the head. When some mechanical thing breaks, it "conks out." If you conk out, you fall asleep deeply and quickly.
I had planned on going out on Friday, but I got home and conked out.
I studied until 4 a.m. and then I conked out.
Hey, wake up, don't conk out on us!

sawing (some) logs: sleeping heavily and snoring. The sound of snoring can be similar to the sound of sawing wood by hand, with long, slow strokes.
Dude, you were really sawing some logs. We had to turn the TV up to drown out the sound.

snore: to breathe noisily while sleeping
Do you snore? Does your husband snore?
His snoring kept me awake all night.

Personality Opposites

always on the go: always doing something, never standing still
I love the weekends because I'm always on the go. I'm never home except to brush my teeth.

homebody: someone who likes to stay home
On the weekends, I'm a homebody. I just like to lounge around the house—watch TV, surf the Internet, take a nap, cook something.

indoors person: someone who prefers to be indoors. They like to do indoor activities, such as watching TV, reading books, surfing the Internet.
I'm an indoor person. I rarely leave home on the weekends.
Stop being such an indoor person. You need to get out, do things, and meet new people.

outdoors person: someone who likes the outdoors
My father is an outdoors person. He loves mountain climbing, jogging, and tennis. I would love to be an outdoor person, but all I do is study in the library.

light sleeper: someone who wakes up easily. If there is any slight noise, they wake up. They cannot sleep with the radio or TV on.
My mother is a light sleeper. I cannot sneak in late.

sleep through anything: a heavy sleeper. They could sleep through a typhoon. They can sleep in a car, train, plane, and subway. They often can sleep standing up.
"Did you feel the earthquake last night?" "There was an earthquake? No. I can sleep through anything."

party animal: a person who likes to stay out late and party
Bill was a party animal right after he got out of the army.

Wow! Jack is a party animal, but he is so shy at work.
Those engineering majors are a bunch of party animals. They study hard and drink hard.

party pooper: someone who wants to go home early from the party; someone who does not want to party
It's only 10 o'clock! Don't be such a party pooper.
My date was a party pooper. Just when things were getting started, she wanted me to take her home.

spontaneous; on the spur of the moment: doing things instantly, without any advance notice. To do things on the spur of the moment is to do something immediately, without thinking about it.
"Are you spontaneous?" "No, I need a week to think about anything major."
She's spontaneous. She's good to go, anywhere, anytime.
He's spontaneous. He proposed on his first date.
"I thought you were going to the movies?" "We decided on the spur of the moment to go shopping instead."

need advance notice: to need to know about something ahead of time in order to be ready for it
"Honey, let's go to the movies tonight." "Tonight? I need some advance notice, please."
Give me a few days' advance notice before you invite your boss to come to our house.

weekend warrior: someone who drinks very heavily, but only on the weekend
Bill's a weekend warrior. You should have seen him last night dancing on the bar.
I was a weekend warrior in college, but not these days.

social drinker: someone who drinks moderate amounts of alcohol for social reasons
In college, I was a weekend warrior, but these days I'm just a social drinker. I only drink at family and work events.

teetotaler: someone who never drinks
My mother is a teetotaler.
"How was your date?" "Kind of a waste of money. The party had free booze, but she was a teetotaler."

3 TECHNOLOGY

Many Korean technology words are taken directly from English, so only a few will be defined here.

bargain shopper; bargain hunter: someone who buys when something is on sale for a bargain
My mother is a bargain shopper. She only shops when there are sales.
I'm a bargain shopper with my own money, but when my mother takes me shopping, that's something else.

impulse buyer; impulse shopper: someone who buys without thinking and often regrets it later
My sister is an impulse shopper. She buys the goofiest stuff, and then takes it back later to get a refund.
"Whoa! Where did you get that hat? A garage sale?" "No, I got it at the mall. I'm just an impulse shopper."

impulsive: acting without thinking
Shy people are seldom impulsive.
You asked her to go away for the weekend on your first date? That was too impulsive. You probably scared her off.

frugal: using money carefully, not wasteful
My grandmother is very frugal. She makes all of her own sauces and grows her own herbs.

thrifty: using money carefully, not spending a lot
James is very thrifty. He always eats at the cafeteria.

cheap: hating or avoiding spending money, like "stingy"
Sam is so cheap. He tries to bring his own drinks into restaurants.

big spender: someone who spends a lot of money
I'm a big spender when I go on vacation. I always spend so much money.

gullible: believing just about anything
My sister is gullible. The used car salesman told her that the car had been owned by a grandmother who only used it to go to church once a week.
My best friend is too gullible. Her husband gets home drunk every night at 2 a.m. smelling of beer and perfume, and she thinks that he was working late.

skeptical: not believing something easily, wanting to see proof before believing
She said her dog ate her homework, but I am skeptical.

She says she slept at a friend's house, but I am skeptical.

instant gratification: getting what you want right away, without waiting
Credit cards allow people to have instant gratification. They don't have to save up for something they want.
I don't want to be rich when I'm 50. I want instant gratification. I want to be rich now.

delayed gratification: having to wait and be patient in order to get what you want
The ability to deal with delayed gratification is important. It's what allows people to work toward a goal.
"Son, when you are older, you will learn the benefits of delayed gratification." "Dad, I hope I never get that old."

technophile: a lover of technology (The ending –phile means "someone who likes/loves.")
My boss is a real technophile. He thinks that every problem can be solved by technology, so we have all the latest technology in our office.

techno-geek; techie: someone who loves technology and knows a lot about it (similar to *technophile*)
My brother is a techo-geek. He has all the new technology.

technophobic / technophobe: having a fear of new technology / someone who is technophobic (The ending -*phobic* means "afraid of.")
My mother is technophobic. She does not trust new technology. She still has her typewriter.
My mother is a technophobe. I bought her a digital camera, but she still uses her old film camera.

4 DATING & NIGHTLIFE

DATING

admire from afar: to secretly admire (like) someone, but keep your distance and not tell them
I've been admiring her from afar, but I've never met her.
I admired her from afar for a month before I asked her out.

baggage: personal problems that may cause trouble in a new relationship
"How was your date?" "He's a nice guy, but he had too much baggage. He had two ex-wives, six kids, a gambling problem, and a drinking problem."

blind date: a date with someone you have never met before
"How was your blind date?" "He was OK, no smash hit. Nothing special."
"Do you like to go on blind dates?" "No, after the last disaster, I swore off blind dates."

break up: to end a relationship
We broke up a year ago.
I want to break up.

cheap date: someone who does not want to spend much money on the date
"How was your date?" "Oh, she was a cheap date; it was great. A couple of beers and a pizza and we were having a good old time."
Jack is a cheap date. His idea of a good time is tteokbokki, a bottle of soju, and a paper cup.

cheap drunk: a personwho gets drunk very quickly, with very little alcohol
"Where do you want to go?" "Oh, I'm a cheap drunk. Let's just go to a beer hof."

cheat on: to be unfaithful to someone you are dating or married to; to date other people while in a relationship
Jane doesn't trust her boyfriend. She always thinks that he will cheat on her.

chemistry: an invisible force that causes an attraction between two people
"How was your blind date?" "He was cute and well-mannered, but there was no chemistry."
"How is your conversation class?" "Great. That class has great chemistry. They are lively, loud, and think everything I say is funny."

crush: an intense attraction to someone, often from afar
"Who was your favorite teacher in high school?" "My music teacher. I had a big crush on him."
"Do you still have a crush on that guy in your math class?" "No, once I met him, the magic was gone."

crushed: brokenhearted from a romance; not just hurt, but crushed, like a used paper cup
"How are you these days?" "After we broke up, I was crushed, but I got over it."
When I caught him cheating on me, I was crushed.
When I didn't get accepted into Yale, I was crushed.

have a crush on: to like someone a lot, often from afar
She always wants to eat at that restaurant because she has a crush on the waiter.

date around: to date a few or many people
After I get to college, I want to date around. I don't want to go steady with the first guy I meet.
Do you think someone should date around before getting married?
My boyfriend said that we should both date around for a while, to make sure that we were right for each other.

"Dear John" letter: a letter from a woman telling a man that the romance is over. You can also get a Dear John phone call or email.
"You look like your dog just died. What's up?"
"Aw, I just got a Dear John letter from my girlfriend."
"What's wrong?" "I just got a Dear John email."

fix up: to arrange a date for two other people
Your brother is cute. Can you fix me up with him?
"Do you know that blonde girl, Mary, in math class?" "Yes, she's my neighbor." "Really? Can you fix me up with her?"
My buddy is fixing me up with one of his co-workers.

flirt: to try to get someone to like you through smiles, looks, speech, and maybe touching
Look at Britney flirting with that new student.
Someone who constantly flirts with a lot of people is called a flirt.
He's a flirt. She says that to everybody.

going steady: dating only one person; in a steady relationship
We've been going steady for six months.
How long have you been going steady?

hit on: to flirt with someone. *I hate going to clubs.*
I just want to dance, not get hit on by every guy.

long-distance romance: a romance in which the two people live far away from each other
"How's your long distance romance going?" "Not too great. I think he's cheating on me."

love at first sight: immediately falling in love the first time you see someone
It was love at first sight. We ended up dating for two years, but I proposed on the first date.
It was love at first sight for me, but it took six months before she would agree to go out on a date with me.

Love is blind. (proverb): When you are in love, you cannot see anything wrong with the person you are in love with.
"Can't he see that she is just using him?" "He should, but love is blind."
I tried to tell her about him, but she did not believe me. Love is blind.

love triangle: a situation in which two people are romantically interested in a third person. Many movies are about love
triangles: *Gone with the Wind, Titanic, Dumb and Dumber*
My boss was caught in a love triangle.
"Have you ever been in a love triangle?" "Well, once there was some overlap between my second and third boyfriend."

lust: sexual desire
You can't love her. You don't even know here. That's not love; it's lust.

make up; kiss and make up: to get back together after a fight or a breakup
Oh, baby, please forgive me. Let's kiss and make up, OK?
"Oh, I see you're back together?" "Yeah, we kissed and made up over the weekend."

mama's boy: a man who is more concerned with pleasing his mother than with pleasing his girlfriend
John was a momma's boy. I got tired of him jumping up and leaving every time she called.

Mr. Right / Miss Right: the perfect, right person to fall in love with
Last night, I met Mr. Right. He's the one.
"Is your new boyfriend Mr. Right?" "No, but he will have to do until Mr. Right comes along."

Opposites attract. (proverb): With personalities, like magnets, opposites are attracted to each other.
"Why did you fix me up with her? We have nothing in common." "I thought, you know, opposites attract. Sorry about that."

Out of sight, out of mind. (proverb): If you do not see your ex- boyfriend or girlfriend for a while, you do not think about them, and therefore, you do not miss them. This helps with mending a broken heart.
"Are you over your boyfriend yet?" "Yeah, he moved to Malaysia. Out of sight, out of mind."

out of your league: above your social level or level of attractiveness, and therefore not likely to be interested in you
"Tom, why didn't you ever marry?" "I guess I was always chasing women who were out of my league."
"Man, I would like to date that new girl in class." "Get real. She is out of your league."

picky: too selective, hard to please. You can be picky about food, or in romance. In romance, it is good to be picky, but if you are too picky, you may end up alone every Saturday night.
"What was wrong with John?" "He was too short."
"What was wrong with Jack?" "He was too poor."
"What was wrong with Jim?" "He was too ugly." "What was wrong with Jerome?" "His name began with a "J""
"You are too picky."

high standards: high expectations; a desire for only the best
"I have high standards. My boyfriend must be at least six feet tall, come from an Ivy League school, and make at least $200,000 a year." "Your standards are too high. You'll never get married."

play Cupid: to act as a matchmaker. According to ancient Roman beliefs, Cupid was a god who shot arrows at people that made them fall in love.
My sister is always trying to play Cupid and fix me up with someone.

play hard to get: to pretend that you don't like someone in order to make them try harder
"Are you still playing hard to get with Jack?"
"Yeah, I'll make him beg a little more, then say 'Yes.'"
"If you play too hard to get he will soon give up."
Britney, I can't tell if you don't like me or you're just playing hard to get.

puppy love: love among very young people that is usually not "true" love and does not last
"Oh, but mama, I love him!" "You're 17 years old. It's only puppy love."
I thought it was the real thing, but it was only puppy love.

secret admirer: someone who secretly has a crush on you, but keeps it secret. They might send you flowers and romantic notes, but not sign their name.
"Wow. Who sent the flowers?" "I don't know. I've got a secret admirer."

soul mate: similar to Mr. and Miss Right, but better; the absolutely perfect mate. Not every couple are soul mates, and they still are happily married.
"Is he your soul mate?" "Oh yes, it's amazing. We have the same favorite movie and song! We feel the same way about everything."

stand up: to promise to meet someone and then not show up
"How was your date?" "She stood me up." "Did she call?" "Nope, nada, nothing."
If you stand me up again, that's it.
Are you standing him up? Are you going to stand him up?
How dare you! Nobody stands me up!

tease: to promise something and not give it on purpose, or to aggravate someone for fun (Teasing is like flirting but not as innocent. A tease is worse than a flirt.
Stop teasing your little brother and give him a cookie.
Stop teasing him. You know you'll never go out with him.
"Wow. Did you see that? I think she likes me." "Not. She's a tease. She does that to everybody."

the silent treatment: not speaking to someone because you are angry at them
I forgot my girlfriend's birthday, and she is giving me the silent treatment. She doesn't answer her phone and doesn't return my calls.
"Why don't you answer your phone?" "I'm giving my boyfriend the silent treatment."
My wife hasn't spoken to me in a week. This is the longest the silent treatment has ever lasted.

two-timer: someone who is unfaithful. They have two girlfriends or boyfriends.
I don't trust him. He's a two-timer.
I caught him two-timing me, so it's over.

unrequited love: one-sided love; love that is not returned
"Is she your new girlfriend?" "I wish. It's more a case of unrequited love. She told me that I'm not her type."
So far, it's unrequited love. She says she just wants to remain friends.

whirlwind romance: a very fast and exciting romance
We had a whirlwind romance. We got married one month after we met.
That's what I call a whirlwind romance. They met on Monday and got married on Friday.

PRECISE RELATIONSHIPS

platonic friend: non-romantic friend
He's just a platonic friend. I've known him since kindergarten.

male friend / female friend: platonic friend; not a boyfriend or girlfriend
She has a lot of male friends, but no boyfriend.

boyfriend, girlfriend: romantic partner (Women sometimes refer to their female platonic friends as their "girlfriends" as well.)
He's going to ask his girlfriend to marry him.
Who's that guy with Kate? Is he her boyfriend or just a male friend?
She loves hanging out with her girlfriends at the coffee shop.

steady boyfriend / girlfriend: someone you are dating steadily, usually for a long time
He's my steady boyfriend.
"Is she your steady girlfriend?" "Yes. We've been going steady for a year."

lover: someone you have sex with
His wife found out that he had a lover and divorced him.
[Some Koreans wrongly use this term, thinking it means "steady boyfriend." On the other hand, the word can be used to describe romantic behavior, as in: *They've been married for five years, but they still act like lovers.*]

PERSONALITY OPPOSITES

affectionate / touchy-feely: liking to show affection (love) / liking to show friendliness or affection through touch
Our new sales director is too touchy-feely. She is always kissing people on the cheek and holding hands and patting backs at every meeting.
"How was your date?" "He was too touchy-feely. I felt uncomfortable. I didn't know him that well."
"Did you meet your fiancée's family?" "Yes, they are very touchy-feely. I got hugged and kissed by every aunt and uncle!"

cold: unaffectionate; showing no emotions; not romantic or sentimental
I know my husband loves me, but he is a very cold person.
I know you dislike your stepfather, but don't be so cold. Go and say hello.
"Why don't you give that beggar some change?"
"He can starve for all I care."
"Oh, that's cold."

cold shoulder: If you give someone the cold shoulder, you ignore them.
I was only trying to ask that pretty girl what time it was, but she gave me the cold shoulder and pretended that she didn't see me.

cold fish: an unemotional, unaffectionate person
My blind date for the football game was a cold fish. She always sat as far away from me as she could.
I can't tell if she's a cold fish or she just doesn't like me.

break up in person: to end a relationship person in person, face to face
"How did you break up with Jack?" "I told him in person. I felt I owed it to him. We dated for over a year."
I broke up in person. I broke up by email.
I broke up by text message.

change your phone number: Some people end relationships in person, and some people just change their phone number! Cold, but effective.
"What did Jack say when you broke up with him?" "I don't know. I just changed my cell phone number and email address."

faithful: loyal or true to someone or something
I was faithful to my boyfriend while he was in the army, but I am not sure if he was faithful to me.
If my husband were ever unfaithful to me, I would divorce him.

playboy / playgirl: someone who is unfaithful as a habit (*Playboy* is a much more common term than *playgirl*.)
I broke up with Jack because he was a playboy.
Don't believe him—he's a playboy.

gigolo: a male escort or prostitute; sometimes used jokingly about a playboy
"Where's Jack?" "That gigolo. I found his address book with the names of about six girls."

Casanova: another slang word for *playboy* (from the name of a famous 17th-century Italian lover)
"Where's Jack?" "That Casanova. I found his address book with the names of about fifty girls."

forgive and forget: to forgive someone quickly and easily, and not talk about it again
If I ever caught my boyfriend cheating on me, I do not know if I could forgive and forget.
You were both unfaithful. Just forgive and forget about it.

hold a grudge: to stay angry at someone; to not forgive someone for a long time
It's been five years. Are you still holding a grudge?
Aw baby, don't hold a grudge. Forgive me.
I'm too nice. I can never hold a grudge for long.

girl-next-door type: an average, nice, ordinary girl
My rich uncle dated a lot of beauty queens, but he eventually married a girl-next-door type.
A lot of guys date sexy girls, but they don't marry them. They marry the girl-next-door type.

femme fatale: a beautiful, sexy female in movies who brings trouble to the men in her life. She uses her beauty and charm to get what she wants out of a man, and then discards him.
That beauty queen was quite a femme fatale. I hear she broke up three marriages.
I'm tired of poor nice guys. I think I'll go for the femme fatale look tonight and get a rich boyfriend.
Men like to date femme fatales, but they generally do not marry them. They marry a nice girl.

lead him/her on, string him/her along: to pretend to like someone
You don't like John. Why do you keep leading him on?
Do you like me, or are you just leading me on so that I'll help you with your homework?
Stop leading her on and tell her that you already have a girlfriend.
How can you string him along like that? You know that he's crazy about you, and you know that you will never love him.

low-maintenance: easy to please; requiring little attention
She's low-maintenance. I call her twice a week, and see her once a week, and she's happy.

high-maintenance: hard to please; requiring a lot of attention
He's high-maintenance. If I don't call him six times a day, he gets upset.
Mary was too high-maintenance. She only wanted to go to the most expensive restaurants; we only did what she wanted to do.

trusting: having faith in people
My wife is not very trusting. She is not the trusting type. When I go on a business trip, she calls me every half hour.
My wife was the trusting type until I came home with lipstick on my collar.

jealous: not trusting of a romantic partner; angry or worried that a romantic partner might be unfaithful
My-ex girlfriend was too jealous. She didn't want me to have female friends.
I think I'll talk to other guys and make my boyfriend jealous.

possessive: very jealous
My ex was too possessive. I could not have my own friends or go anywhere without him.
He was too possessive. He acted like he owned me.

DRINKING
DRINKING WORDS

black out: to lose your memory of certain period of time due to heavy drinking (Koreans say "cut the film.")
Have you ever blacked out while drinking?
I blacked out for about two hours and woke up on my bedroom floor.

pass out: to lose consciousness from drinking
Pass out is also used for non-drinking reasons, like too much heat, exercise, or fear.
She passed out when she saw all that blood.
He was overcome by the gas fumes, and he passed out.
But we are talking about drinking, so:
Bob's passed out in the back. No more chug-a-lugging for him.
Last night, I drank straight bourbon and passed out.

havea buzz: to be at a happy point in drinking; not drunk, but beginning to feel the effects of alcohol
"Oh, that tastes good. I needed that. How are you doing?" "Cold beer, hot music—I've got a buzz."
"What are you grinning at? Are you drunk?" "Not yet, but I've got a buzz."

tipsy: slightly drunk
No more for me; I'm getting tipsy.

Oh, look—mom's a little tipsy from the champagne.
I was not drunk last night; I was tipsy.

drunk: in a stupid condition from drinking too much alcohol (also: a person who drinks too much; an alcoholic)
"Look—Jack is drunk." "Again? Jack is a drunk."

inebriated; intoxicated: drunk
Jack got inebriated at the company party.
He was intoxicated, so I left when he wasn't looking.

blitzed; bombed; sloshed; smashed: (slang) very drunk
Jack was blitzed at the party.
No more drinks for me; I don't want to get smashed.

The room is spinning. If you drink too much, or too fast, you may get dizzy. It appears that the room is spinning.
Whoa. Somebody stop the room from spinning. I'm getting dizzy.
"How do you feel?" "Awful, the room is spinning. Where's the bathroom? Quick."

hangover / hung over: the bad feeling that you have the morning after you drink heavily / having a hangover
I have a hangover. I'm hung over.

nursing a hangover: moving slowly and carefully the morning after a night of heavy drinking
"Why didn't Jack come to church?" "He's at home nursing a hangover."

slurring (your words): unclear in your speech because of drinking alcohol
"Let's go home, you're starting to slur your words." "Thashhh not twue."
That drunk was slurring so much that he could not even tell the cop his name.

throw up; vomit; upchuck; barf: when your food or drink comes back out of your stomach and up through your mouth
I feel like I'm going to throw up.
Jack threw up after two bottles of soju.
Jack upchucked in my car. He barfed all over the seat.

PERSONALITY OPPOSITES

belle of the ball: the most popular person (usually female) at a social event, such as a party or dance
I was the belle of the ball last night at the company party.
Oh mom, I was the belle of the ball! Seven boys asked me to dance, and they also asked for my phone number.

wallflower: a shy person who does not dance or participate at a party
Don't be such a wallflower. Get out there and dance.
"How was the nightclub?" "Not so good. I was a wallflower. I just couldn't get in the mood."
"How was the party?" "Not fun. I was a wallflower, and I just sat by myself all night."

binge drinker: someone who does not drink often, but when they do drink, they drink very much; a heavy drinker, but not necessarily a frequent drinker. Binge drinking is a problem for many college students, especially freshmen.
My college roommate was a binge drinker. He only drank about once a month, but when he did drink, he always got drunk and threw up.
A major cause of binge drinking is that many college bars offer two drinks for the price of one on Friday afternoons.

teetotaler: someone who never drinks
My mother is a teetotaler.
"How was your date?" "Kind of a waste of money. The party had free booze, but she was a teetotaler."

early bird: someone who gets up very early
My father is an early bird. He's up at 5 every morning and jogs three miles before anybody else wakes up.
"The early bird catches the worm" is a common saying that means good things happen to people who wake up early.
"I got to the sale at noon, but they were already sold out." "Well, the early bird catches the worm."

night owl: someone who stays out, or up, very late
My sister is a night owl. She stays up until 4 every night.
I'm a night owl during semester breaks. Sometimes, I get home after sunup.

happy drunk: someone who gets very happy when they drink
"Jack, do you mind if my cousin comes with us?" "No, I like him. He's a happy drunk."

mean drunk; unhappy drunk: a person who gets angry, mean, rude, or unpleasant when they drink
He's a nice guy when he's sober, but he's a mean drunk. So I broke up with him.

He was a fun date until he started drinking. He's a mean drunk. I hate that.

high tolerance: the ability to drink a lot of alcohol easily without showing the effects
I have a high tolerance. I can drink 4 bottles of soju by myself.

low tolerance: the inability to drink much alcohol without showing the effects
What? Your face turns red after one shot of soju? You have a low tolerance for alcohol.

life of the party: the most entertaining, the funniest, the most lively person at a party
Jack was the life of the party. I never knew he was so funny.
He was kind of quiet at first, but after he started drinking, he was the life of the party.

wet blanket: a person who takes the excitement out of the evening (A good way to put out a small fire is to throw a wet blanket on it. A person who is unenthusiastic or in a bad mood, who puts the whole party in a bad mood is a wet blanket. They put out the fire, the excitement, of the party.)
"You guys drink too much." "Aw, don't be such a wet blanket."
"How was your date?" "She was a wet blanket. Every time we thought of something fun to do, she said no. She didn't drink or smoke or even talk much. She just sat there looking bored. She was kind of a wet blanket."

party animal: a person who likes to stay out late and party
"Who's the party animal?" "That's Bill. He just got out of the army."
Wow. Jack is a real party animal. He is so shy at work.
Those engineering majors are a bunch of party animals. They study hard and drink hard.

party pooper: someone who wants to go home early from the party; someone who does not want to party
"I'll see you guys tomorrow." "It's only 10 o'clock! Don't be such a party pooper."
"How was your date?" "She was a party pooper. Just when things were getting started, she wanted to go home."

weekend warrior: a person who drinks a lot, but only on the weekends

social drinker: someone who rarely drinks, usually only on social occasions, such as weddings (When Koreans say "social drinker," they mean a person who drinks socially, regularly.)
"Do you like to drink?" "Not really, I'm more of a social drinker. When my friends drink, I usually just have one beer and sip it all night."
My sister is a social drinker. She drinks every now and then, but never very much—usually only at weddings.

5 SOFA TIME

You already know many of the TV terms, so they are not included here. They are included in the unit to jog your memory (help you remember).

TV TERMS

bloopers: mistakes in a movie or TV show that are usually funny
At the end of Rush Hour 2 with Jackie Chan, they show about five minutes of bloopers.
The bloopers were funnier than the movie itself.

channel surfer: someone who changes the channels often (People who hate commercials often start surfing whenever a commercial comes on.)
Stop surfing the channels and stay on one program.
My brother is a channel surfer, and it drives me crazy.

commercial: a television advertisement (Koreans use "CF.")
I hate those coffee commercials where good-looking people start sipping coffee and look so beautiful and content.

freeze frame: stop the action; also, a pause button (They do this during disputed calls in soccer, baseball, and tennis.)
Whoa, right there. Hit the freeze frame.

laugh track: a sound track of people laughing in a sitcom
Their laugh track is too much. That stuff is not that funny. And they are laughing in the wrong places.

lipy-sync: to pretend to sing, but actually to just move your lips along with the song (If something is synchronized, it is in sync, in unison with something else. On TV, most singers lip-sync.)
His dancing is OK, but his lip-syncing is awful.

prime time (not golden time): the time when people watch the most TV, from 7 to 10 p.m. Thus, advertisers must pay the most money for commercials at this time. If an afternoon program is very popular, they might move it to prime time.
That show is too sexy. They should not be showing it in prime time.

repeat; rerun: a program that has been shown before and is being shown again
Great, my first night off in a week and every show is a rerun. Every show is a repeat.

MC: master of ceremonies; host
Who's the MC of the awards show this year?

talk show: a show that only or mostly involves famous people being interviewed
"Who is she, and why is she on all the talk shows?" "That's the author of the Harry Potter series. She's promoting her latest book."

trash TV: programs about trashy, sexy topics
There's too much trash TV these days.
There's nothing but trash (bad quality) on TV these days.

6 HEALTH & FITNESS

ache: to hurt; a constant, low or mid-level pain (headache / earache / stomachache)
Oh, I ate too much chocolate. I have a stomachache.
After moving all those boxes, my back really aches.

addiction / addict: the condition of being habitually dependent on something like drugs or gambling / a person who shows such a condition
He used to be a nice kid, but his addiction to drugs has made him do bad things. Last week, he robbed that convenience store.

allergic / allergic reaction: having an allergy / a negative, sometimes dangerous reaction that a person's body has to some material that has entered or come in contact with it, such as dog hair, flower pollen, food, or medication
She almost died when she had an allergic reaction to the peanuts in that candy.

allergy: the conditionof a person's body having a negative reaction if exposed to a certain material
My sister has an allergy to cats. She always sneezes if there is a cat nearby.

blister: a liquid-filled bubble that forms on a person's skin because of too much rubbing
She got a blister on her thumb from playing tennis all day.
These new shoes are giving me blisters on my ankles.

blood / bleed: the red liquid that flows through a person's body / to have blood come out of one's body
My arm was bleeding quite a lot after the dog bit me.

blood type: one of four categories of human blood
His blood type is B, so I think we would make a good couple.
If you get blood in a hospital, it must be the same blood type as yours.

boil: like a large pimple occurring anywhere on the body
I have a boil on my foot, and it hurts to wear shoes.

bruised; black and blue: having discoloration of the skin (often blackish or bluish) caused by an injury or hard contact
I fell down the stairs and bruised my leg. It has been black and blue for a week.

burned: damaged by heat or fire
Ouch! I just burned my tongue on this hot soup.
He burned his hand when he tried to help his mother cook dinner.

cancer: a serious disease that grows slowly inside the body
Because he smoked cigarettes every day for twenty years, he developed lung cancer.

cast: a hard, protective casing made from plaster that is put over broken bones to stop them from moving and allow them to heal
All of my classmates signed their names on my cast when I broke my leg.

crutch: a long, narrow triangular frame of wood or metal that fits under a person's arm to help them walk with a damaged leg or foot
It took me a few days to get used to walking with crutches after I broke my ankle, but it's easy now.

checkup: a regular examination by a doctor or dentist to make sure everything is fine(Note: this is not a examination that is done when someone is sick or has a problem.)

It's been six months since I went to the dentist. I think I should schedule a check up next week.

clinic: a place where people go to see a doctor. It is smaller than a hospital, but bigger than a doctor's office.
If you are feeling sick, you should go to the school clinic. They might be able to give you some medicine.

cold: a minor illness that can cause a sore throat, sneezing, and coughing
I didn't go to work yesterday because I had a cold.

flu: a potentially dangerous illness caused by bacteria that produces symptoms like a bad cold
I think you have the flu. You should go see a doctor.

pneumonia: a serious lung infection that often results from the body temperature dropping too low
She had to stay in bed for two weeks because of pneumonia.

cold turkey: suddenly and completely (in reference to stopping a bad habit)
When my grandfather died from lung cancer, I decided to quit cold turkey. I haven't touched a cigarette since.

CPR: stands for Cardio-Pulmonary-Resuscitation; a technique to start a person's heart and lungs working again if they have stopped working
To perform CPR on someone who has had a heart attack, you should firmly press down on the chest four times and then breathe into the person's mouth four times.

diarrhea: a sickness that makes food travel quickly through the bowels and come out as a liquid
There must have been something wrong with that seafood we had for lunch. Now, we all have diarrhea.

dizzy: lightheaded; feeling unstable while standing or walking, like the room is spinning
He felt dizzy after going on some of the rides at Everland last week. / I think I might be getting a fever. I feel really dizzy.

drugs: chemicals that affect the body, including medicines and illegal drugs such as cocaine or marijuana
The doctor gave me some drugs to help my stomachache, but they aren't working. It still hurts.

drugstore / druggist: a pharmacy, or store that sells medicine / a pharmacist or person who prepares medicine in a drugstore
Is there a drugstore near campus? I need to buy some cough syrup.
She's studying to become a druggist.

pharmacy / pharmacist: a drugstore or store that sells medicine / a druggist, or person who prepares medicine in a drugstore
Is there a pharmacy near campus? I need to buy some cough syrup.
She's studying to become a pharmacist.

emergency room (ER): the part of the hospital where people go for sudden or serious health issues. *Working in an emergency room has to be a stressful job. ER doctors have to deal with so many people and problems every day.*

faint; pass out; black out: to lose consciousness; "black out" can also mean to lose memory of a certain period of time
She fainted when she saw how badly he was bleeding.
He drank so much soju that he passed out at 10 o'clock last night.

fever: an abnormally high body temperature, above 37°C (98.6°F)
Could you take my temperature? I think I have a fever. My head is burning up.

give blood; donate blood: to allow a doctor or nurse to take some of your blood, which they will keep and then give to another person who needs it
Do you see that white bus with the red cross on it? You can give blood there. They'll even give you a free cookie.

Intensive Care Unit (ICU): an area in a hospital for patients who are seriously hurt or sick and need constant care and attention
My father was in ICU for a week after his heart attack, but they've moved him into a regular room now. He's going to be okay.

itch: a strange, ticklish feeling somewhere on the body that requires scratching to feel better
That mosquito bite is giving me such an itch. I can't stand it.

nauseous; nauseated: feeling dizzy and like a person who is about to throw up
The smell of bad eggs makes me nauseous.

pain: hurt, ache, or a very uncomfortable feeling
She feels a lot of pain in her back. I think it's because she is always picking up her young son.

paralyzed: unable to move due to an injury (usually to the spine) or illness
After the car accident, he was paralyzed from the waist down. He never walked again.

pimple; zit; acne: a small, boil-like sore commonly occurring on the faces of teenagers
Oh no! I have a blind date tonight, and now I have a big zit on my nose.

pollen: small particles that come from flowers, trees, and plants
My allergies are killing me. The pollen is causing me to sneeze every few minutes.

prescription: a written order for special medicine given by a doctor
The doctor gave her a prescription for some strong antibiotics to try to fight her infection.

prescription drug: strong medicine that people can only buy with a special order written by a doctor
I can't sell you that medicine without doctor's orders. It's a prescription drug.

pull a muscle: to accidentally stretch a muscle too far, causing pain and tearing
He pulled a muscle in his leg during the football game. Now, he has to rest for a while.

rash: a section of skin that has become red, bumpy, and itchy; is usually caused from too much rubbing or an allergic reaction
You have to wear pants in this forest. There is poison ivy that will give your legs a bad rash if your skin touches it.

rehabilitation or **rehab:** the process of healing damaged limbs, muscles, or even minds
He was in rehab with a physical therapist for 6 months after the car accident. Now, he can walk fine.

runs in the family: passed on from parents to their children in their genes
Heart disease runs in my family.
Breast cancer runs in her family, so she gets checked every six months.

scab: a layer of dried blood that forms over a cut
This scab on my knee is from falling off my bike.

scar: a permanent mark left on the skin from a large cut
This scar on my side is from my kidney transplant.
He was physically OK after the war, but he had a lot of mental and emotional scars.

seasick: throwing up or feeling nauseous from the motion of a boat
Our boat got caught in some rough weather and I got seasick.

shot; injection: medicine given by placing a needle into the skin and squeezing a liquid into the body
I think I'm going to get a flu shot this fall so I don't get sick this winter.

sinuses: hollow spaces in a person's head, below the eyes and behind the nose, that can be affected by allergies
I feel tired and dizzy because of my sinus allergy.

sore: in pain; aching
Yesterday was my first workout in months. I'm so sore now.

sore throat: pain in the throat because of a cold or too much coughing
I have a sore throat. Could you get me some cough syrup?

sprain: a joint, like the ankle or wrist, that gets swollen and painful because it is bent too far; to bend a joint to far, causing pain and swelling
I sprained my ankle playing tennis. Now, it's quite swollen. I'm going to put ice on it.

stitches: nylon or metal thread used to sew together the skin around a deep cut to help it heal
The hockey player needed twenty-two stitches in his face after he was cut by the other player's skate.

stomachache; stomach cramps: pain felt in the stomach from bad food or illness
I don't know what was in that soup, but I have a bad stomachache now.

swell: to grow bigger because of an injury, illness, or allergic reaction
Uh oh, my throat is swelling. I think I ate a peanut, and I'm allergic to them. Please take me to the hospital.

swollen: the state of something being made larger due to injury
My ankle is swollen because I sprained it at tennis practice today.

tendon / ligament: a string-like tissue that attaches muscles to joints or bones
Ow! I think I just tore a tendon in my arm.

throw up; vomit; upchuck; barf: to eject food and drink from the stomach through the mouth
He drank too much beer and then barfed all over my car!

tonsils: small, rounded tissue on both sides of the throat at the back of a person's mouth
I had my tonsils removed when I was a kid. I remember having to eat a lot of ice cream because of the swelling.

EYES

contact lenses (contacts): small plastic discs that are placed directly onto the eyeball in order to correct vision problems
For athletes, wearing contacts is a much better option than wearing glasses.

TEETH

braces: small metal wires put on teeth to straighten them
I hated wearing braces when I was a kid, but now I'm glad to have straight teeth.

cavity: a hole in a tooth
I had to get four cavities filled by the dentist today. I hated it.

toothache: pain felt in the teeth and gums
You should go to the dentist. You keep complaining about a toothache.

wisdom teeth: the teeth farthest back in the mouth that grow in most people in their late teens or early twenties
The dentist told me I should get my wisdom teeth pulled out, but I'm afraid it will hurt.

HOSPITAL STAFF

nurse; RN; LPN: a person who works in a hospital to take care of sick patients and assist doctors (RN = registered nurse; LPN = licensed practical nurse)
My mother is an RN. She's the head nurse at Jaesang Hospital.

physical therapist: a person who helps people strengthen their muscles and improve their flexibility after an injury
After three years of working with a physical therapist, John could finally walk normally again.

respiratory therapist: a specialist who helps people with breathing problems
A respiratory therapist helped Mary get better after her bout with pneumonia.

X-ray technician: a person who operates the machinery that takes X-ray images
As an X-ray technician, he sees a lot of people with broken bones.

7 HOLIDAYS & FESTIVALS

EMOTIONS & MOODS

aggravating; annoying; irritating: causing a slight feeling of anger or frustration
That scratching sound is irritating.
It's annoying when cell phones go off during a movie. If it happens too many times, it is really aggravating.

anxious; nervous: worried or scared that something bad might happen
I am always nervous before a big exam.
My mother-in-law makes me nervous.

ashamed: very embarrassed, usually about something serious
She was ashamed when she was arrested for shoplifting.

burned out or **burnt out:** mentally or physically exhausted
I was burnt out after high school. I did not feel like studying in college until my junior year.
I'm taking a break this weekend. I worked seventy hours last week, and I am burnt out.

confused: unable to understand or to think clearly
I'm confused. Do we turn here or at the next exit? The map isn't clear.

depressed: very sad
I'm depressed. My boyfriend went into the army last month, my best friend went to Australia for the summer, and it's been raining all week.

have (got) the blues: (slang) to be depressed
I've got the blues. My boyfriend went into the army.

drained: very tired. mentally or physically, or both
That is the last time I baby sit for twins. I'm drained.

dread: to be worried about or afraid of something in the future
On Friday afternoon, I look forward to the weekend. On Sunday night, I dread going back to work.

embarrassed: feeling stupid or uncomfortable in front of other people
I was embarrassed when my cell phone rang in class.

envy: to want something that someone else has; to feel envious of
Are you envious because she's so talented? Do you envy her?

exhausted: very tired *I'm exhausted.*
That was my last marathon.

furious: very angry
She was furious when she found out that he bought a fishing boat.
He was so furious that he threw his computer out the window.

grouchy; cranky: irritable, in a bad mood
Bill is not a morning person. He is always cranky in the morning. It's not until after lunch that he stops being so grouchy.

in a funk: sad or depressed for a long time
She's been in a funk for a month since her boyfriend went abroad to study.
I'm in a funk. I lost my job, and my car was stolen.
She's in a funk. All her friends have dates for the dance, but she doesn't.

jealous: envious; or angry because you think your boyfriend or girlfriend might be unfaithful
She always gets the highest grade without even studying. I'm so jealous.
Amy's boyfriend gets jealous when she flirts with other guys.

kick back; relax; mellow out: to rest
I'm going to stay home and relax this weekend.
Let's kick back and order a pizza and watch TV tonight.
That was a stressful week at work. I'm going to stay home and mellow out this weekend.
Mellow out. You worry too much.

knock your socks off: to impress; to be outstanding
"How was the movie?" "It'll knock your socks off."

monotonous: very boring because it is always the same
"What's your job like?" "Monotonous. I just type all day."

tedious: monotonous and tiring
Computer programming became tedious after a few years. My next job will be in sales. I want to meet people.
This is tedious. I need a break.

moody: changing moods quickly and unpredictably; often in a bad mood
I didn't date her long. She was too moody. I never know what mood she would show up in.
She was moody. When she was happy, she was very happy. But that was only 10% of the time. The other 90% she was grouchy.

pout: to pretend to be very said when you are really just a little sad
Stop pouting. I didn't yell at you, I was yelling at the computer.
No ice cream until you finish your homework. Now stop pouting and go do it.
Stop that or I'll give you something to pout about!

proud: very satisfied about doing something or with yourself; feeling pride
You should be proud of yourself. Getting an A+ in that class isn't easy.

recharged: energized; having energy again
I work at home and usually start getting tired around 4, so I take a nap and wake up feeling recharged.
That sauna really recharged me.

relaxing: restful; soothing
That music is very relaxing. Is it Mozart?
Vacations with my in-laws are not very relaxing.

relieved: happy that something you were worried about did not happen
I was so relieved when I found out that he wasn't hurt.
She was relieved when she found out her final grade was a B, not a D.

get revenge: to harm another person because they have harmed you
My sister lost my bracelet, so I will get revenge by hiding her ring.
He lied to me. I want revenge. I want to get revenge.

sick and tired: to be upset and no longer patient about something
I'm sick and tired of always cleaning up after my roommate. He's so messy.

soothing: relaxing, especially for someone who is upset or stressed
I like to take hot baths. I find them very soothing after a long day of classes.
Her baby was cranky, so she played some soothing music.

stressed (out): unhappy because of mental pressure
My job gives me stress. I am stressed at work.
My job stresses me out. I am stressed out at work.
I commute an hour and a half each way to work every day. But I don't mind, because by the time I get home I am no longer stressed out.

have a temper tantrum; have a fit; throw a fit: to become so angry that you lose control (When a young child is very upset, and he kicks and screams and jumps and cries, he is having a temper tantrum.)
A child at the table next to us had a temper tantrum and ruined our meal.
She had a fit when I tried to put her to bed.

tick off: (slang) to make angry
Why are you always late? You know that ticks me off.
I'm ticked off, and I'm going to stay ticked off until you apologize.
It ticks me off when some loud-mouthed guy in a restaurant keeps talking on his cell phone.

tickled pink: very happy (When you tickle a baby, they start laughing, blood goes to their face, and they turn pink.)
I was tickled pink when I opened my present.
I wasn't just happy—I was tickled pink.
I got an F on my mid-term exam, so I was tickled pink to get an A on the final.

tranquil: very relaxed or relaxing; serene
I had a tranquil vacation. We rented a secluded cabin by the lake.
Disneyland was fun, but it definitely was not tranquil.

yuck: a word used to express disgust
Oh, yuck! You actually eat that?

gross: (slang) disgusting
I can't believe you set me up on a blind date with him. He was so gross.

8 WORKING & GETTING THERE

WORKPLACE PERSONALITY OPPOSITES

boss from hell: a very mean boss
I have a boss from hell. Nothing pleases him. He's a cruel dictator

pushover: a very easygoing and weak person (i.e., someone who is easy to "push over")
My new boss is a pushover. I come in late all the time, and he believes every excuse.
Jack, you're a pushover. You should start being stricter with your employees.

boss's pet: the boss's favorite worker, who receives special treatment
Watch out for her. She's the boss's pet. If you say anything bad about the boss in front of her, she'll run and tell him.
I am not the boss's pet. I am just very good at my job. That's why I get better treatment.

in the doghouse: in trouble with your spouse or boss because of something you did wrong
He's in the doghouse because he forgot his wife's birthday. He's sleeping on the couch.
Oh no, my boss told me to mail these letters by express mail today, and I forgot. I'll be in the doghouse again.

brownnose: to try to get the approval of someone important by flattering them or doing favors for them; to be a brownnoser (Often, the teacher's or boss's pet is a brownnoser.)
She's brownnosing the teacher because she wants a good grade.

He always compliments the boss on her clothes. What a brownnoser!

badmouth: to say bad things about someone or something
My mother-in-law is always badmouthing me to the rest of the family.

by the book: in the proper and usual way; according to the rules
My boss is conservative. He does things by the book. Nothing fancy.

loose cannon: a person who does not follow the rules
Don't put him in charge. He's a loose cannon. Instead of renting a car, he might buy one.
Jack's energetic and a hard worker, but he's a loose cannon. He needs a lot of supervision.

unguided missile: a modern term for "loose cannon." If a missile is unguided, it can go anywhere.
He bought the wrong stocks! What's wrong with him? He's an unguided missile. But he got a great price!

career track / mommy track: In some cases, a woman in the workplace has two choices: The career track means long hours, travel, advanced training, and promotions. The mommy track is shorter working hours with no overtime, weekend work, or travel, and less chance of promotion, in order to take care of children.
After you graduate, do you want to go on the mommy track or the career track?
I'm thinking the career track before I have kids, and the mommy track after.

company man: a person who is loyal to a company and likes the security of a company job, and who therefore who does not break the rules or take risks
My father has worked for the same company for twentyyears. He's a company man.
I don't want to be a company man for the rest of my life. I want to start my own business someday.

entrepreneur: a risk taker who starts a new business when the opportunity arises, or several new businesses.
My brother is an entrepreneur. His first two businesses failed, but his third one is very successful.
To get the economy going again, we need to make it easier for entrepreneurs to start new businesses.

happy camper: a person who is happy and cheerful, even when events are unpleasant
I wish I were more like Britney. She's always such a happy camper.
Jack's a happy camper. Nothing ever bothers him.

malcontent: a person who is unhappy most of the time; a person who complains a lot
Jack's a malcontent. He complains about everything. If we leave him on that work team, he will start making everyone else unhappy.
Jane's a moody, malcontented worker. We tried talking to her, but she complained about that also.

have your act together: to be efficient and well-organized; to know what you are doing; to be competent
Wow. Our new professor has his act together. He plans every minute of every class.

disorganized: not in order; not planned well; not organized
Kate is so disorganized. She never knows where her stuff is.

get your act together: improve your behavior; become more competent and organized
Nobody did their homework? You had better get your act together, or everyone will flunk.
Your test is tomorrow. Get your act together! Turn off the TV and study.

idea person: a person who is good at coming up with big, creative ideas, but not at carrying them out in detail
I'm an idea person.The details bore me.

detail person: a person who is good at taking care of every detail
My sister is not creative, but she is a great detail person. She'd make a good accountant.

lone wolf: a loner who prefers to do things alone rather than on a project with others; not a people person
Jack is a bit of a lone wolf, so I try to find him projects that he can do alone.
I would prefer to be a lone wolf on this project. A partner would just slow me down.

team player: someone who works well within a team and gets along well with others
Your lone-wolf days are over. Either become a team player, or you're out of here.
Jack's a team player. He's a joy to work with.

people person: someone who likes, and is good at, dealing with people, and likes meeting new people
I'm a people person, so I would like to be in sales.
Jack is the best in the department, and he is next in line for promotion. But he's just not a people person.
We need to have a people person in charge of customer relations.

hermit: a stronger form of loner; a person who is anti-social (dislikes people and wants little or no contact with them); often used as an exaggeration
Jack's too anti-social to be a good manager.
Stop acting anti-social and go mingle.
Last weekend, I was a hermit. I stayed home and did nothing. I don't mean to be anti-social, but we had better get back to work.

queen bee: a powerful, bossy person (like the queen of a beehive), usually a woman
I'm the queen bee in my department.
I don't like her. She's too much of a queen bee.

worker bee: an average, low-level employee
I'm not a boss. I'm just a worker bee.
I kind of miss being a worker bee. Now that I'm a manager, I have too many responsibilities.
Are you a manager or a worker bee?

self-starter: someone with initiative and energy; someone who is self-motivated
I'm energetic. I'm a self-starter. I get things done.
This job involves sales. Only self-starters need apply.

watching the clock: spending more time looking at the clock than working; looking forward to the end of the workday
Stop watching the clock and get some work done!
"How's it going today?" "Oh, the boss is away, and work is slow, so I'm mainly just watching the clock."

top dog: the highest-ranking person
Who's top dog around here? Who's the top dog?
Jack's top dog in sales this month.
I want to have my own company and be top dog.

low man on the totem pole: the lowest ranking person
"Where are you in your department?" "I just started working there, so I'm low man on the totem pole."
Bill Gates is top dog at Microsoft, and some janitor is low man on the totem pole.

workaholic: someone who works a lot. They may love their job or may not. Either way, they work very much.
"Is your father a workaholic?" "Yeah, he has his own business, and he works all the time. He brings his notebook computer with him when we go on a picnic."
It's easy to be a workaholic if you love your work, but otherwise, it's a drag.

slacker / slack off: someone who does not work hard and does not know what they want to do with their life / to be lazy; to not work hard be lazy, to not work hard.
"What does your brother do?" "He's a slacker. He has a master's degree in computers, and he works part time in a video store. His full time job is watching TV."
Stop slacking off. Get back to work.
Sales are down. Our salesmen must be slacking off.

BUSINESS IDIOMS
WORKPLACE RANKING

flunky: a low-ranking person who takes orders from others
I'm tired of being a flunky. I want to go back to college and get a better job.
I worked as a flunky at a construction site.

gofer: a flunky who gets things and runs errands, from "go for" = "go and get"
"How's your new job?" "Aw, I am supposed to be a secretary, but I'm really just a gofer."
He was a gofer at the record company until they heard him singing one day; now he's a star.

grunt: someone who does all the hard, boring, low-level work
Ted has dreams of being a boss, but for now, he's just a grunt.

suit: an important person of some power; a middle- to high-ranking executive
"Where were you last night?" "I had a meeting with the suits."

big wheel: an important person
What does your brother do at Intel? He's a big wheel. He's in charge of hiring and firing in all their Asia plants.
Flying with my brother in his corporate jet always makes me feel like a big wheel.

big boss; top dog: the person in charge
Everyone wants to be the big boss, but it takes a lot of work to be top dog.

MANAGEMENT STYLES

carrot and stick: the use of reward and punishment to motivate workers: reward (carrot) and punishment (stick)
Let's try the carrot and stick approach. We will promise them a bonus if they succeed, and threaten to fire them if they fail.
Management is using the old carrot and stick.
Try less carrot and more stick next time.

hands-on: actively involved in the everyday activities of employees; supervising employees closely
I intend to be a hands-on manager. If you need me, you can reach me anytime on my cell phone.

hands-off: not interfering with or closely supervising employees; letting employees make their own decisions
I like his hands-off management style. It encourages initiative.

COMMUNICATION

networking: making contacts with other people in your field or area of interest; often used in connection with looking for a job or finding out information
I'll do some networking and see if I can get some interviews.
You'll never find a job online. You should try networking.

on the same page: being in agreement, sharing understanding or opinion
Are we all on the same page?
"Jack, was there something you didn't understand?" "No, I've got it now. We're on the same page."

INDEPENDENT

entrepreneur: a risk-taker who starts a new business when the opportunity arises
My brother is an entrepreneur. His first two businesses failed, but his third one is very successful.
To get the economy going again, we need to make it easier for entrepreneurs to start new businesses.

freelance: working on different jobs for short periods of time rather than working long-term for one employer; also, a person who works freelance
He works freelance, mainly for banks.
I'd like to quit this job and work freelance.
He's a freelance illustrator.

self-employed: working for yourself; owning
I'm self-employed.
He's a self-employed architect.

TRANSPORTATION

Most of the transportation vocabulary targets are not idioms, so they will not be defined.

highway: a big road that connects cities
Highway 1 connects Seoul and Busan.

expressway: a highway that drivers can only get on or off at certain places
It is easy to get there. Just take the expressway and get off at exit 4.

breakdown: a vehicle suddenly failing to work because of a mechanical problem
There was a breakdown on Highway 90. It caused a huge traffic jam.

bridge: a structure that connects two pieces of land that are divided
Seoul has many interesting bridges. I like the Banpo Bridge the most.

bumper to bumper: heavy traffic; literally means the front of one car is touching the back of the car in front of it
Highway 1 is always bumper-to-bumper. It is like a parking lot.

bus lane: the lane that only buses can use
James got a ticket for driving in the bus lane. That is going to cost him a lot of money.

fast lane: the far left-hand lane, which is intended for driving at higher speeds
Get into the fast lane.
I hate it when slow drivers stay in the fast lane.

commute: to use some form of transportation to get to work or school; the trip to work or school
The new subway line makes it easier for many people to commute.
I have a two-hour commute every day.

designated driver: the person who is selected, or designated, not to drink so that they can drive the others in a group
OK. Whose turn is it to be the designated driver?

DWI (driving while intoxicated; DUI (driving under the influence of alcohol): the offense you are charged with if you are arrested for drunk driving
Jack got a DWI last night. Jack got a DUI.
Jack was arrested for DWI. Jack was charged with DUI.

fender-bender: a minor car accident without serious damage or injuries
I'm fine; it was just a fender-bender.

flat tire: a tire with a hole in it that lets the air out
Oh great, a flat tire. We'll be late big time.

gasoline or **gas:** the liquid fuel used in most cars; petrol
We need some gas, stop at the next station.
Gas is getting expensive. My truck is not gas—it's diesel.

gas-guzzler: a vehicle that uses a lot of gas and gets very few miles per gallon or liter; for example, a big SUV or Humvee
My car is a gas-guzzler. With the higher gas prices, I think I'll trade it in on something smaller.

Global Positional System (GPS): a device in most cars that shows your location and helps you find places
My taxi had a GPS.

hand-me-down car: When your mother makes you wear your older brother's clothes, you are wearing hand-me-down clothes.
When your mother gets a new car and gives you her old car, you got a hand-me-down car.
"Did you buy this new?" "No, it was a hand-me-down from my mother."

hitchhike: to stand by the road with your thumb in the air and hope that someone stops and gives you a ride
Let's save money and hitchhike.
Hitchhiking can be dangerous.
Do you want to pick up that hitchhiker?

intersection: the place where two or more roads cross
Meet me at the intersection in front of school.

lost: not knowing where you are precisely, and/or not knowing how to get to your destination
You're lost, so pull over and ask for directions.

main drag: the biggest and most important street in a particular area
Go straight until you hit the main drag and turn right.

map: a picture that shows land features and roads.
My father prefers to use a map, but I like to use my GPS.

ride shotgun: slang for riding in the front passenger seat (If three or four people are going somewhere in a car, somebody other than the driver might yell, "I got shotgun!" or just "Shotgun!" meaning they want to sit in the front.)
"Who drove, you or your father?" "My father drove, and I rode shotgun with the map."

rush hour: the time or times of day when traffic is heaviest
My mom and dad always leave for work early. They drive and want to avoid rush hour.

shortcut: a quicker way to get somewhere
Turn right, I know a shortcut.
There's a shortcut through the mountains, but it looks like the road is narrow.

shuttle bus: a bus that goes back and forth over the same (usually short) route
Is there a shuttle bus from the hotel to the airport?

tollroad: a road with toll booths at which drivers must stop and pay money
Slow down as you approach the toll booth. I have to get my money out.
The toll road is shorter. And more expensive.

totaled: (of a car) completely ruined; unable to be repaired
It was a bad accident. Both cars were totaled.
I totaled my car last week. My car was totaled.

traffic jam: when cars move slowly or not at all because of congestion
I was late to work because my bus got stuck in a traffic jam.

traffic ticket: a fine for breaking a traffic law
I have three traffic tickets on my record, but none of them are speeding tickets.

transfer: to change subway lines or buses
It is easy to get there from here. Just transfer at Seoul Station.

underground parking: parking lots below ground level
Many stores and buildings in Korea have underground parking.

(within) walking distance: close enough to walk to
"How do you get to school?" "I live within walking distance."
The subway is not within walking distance of my apartment, so I take the shuttle bus.

wreck; accident: an incident in which one or more cars are damaged and people may be injured
There was a wreck on highway 90 that blocked traffic for an hour.
We were in a traffic accident on our way home from skiing.

15 BOARD GAMES
BOARD GAME CONSTRUCTION

The next eight pages are two board games.
1. Cut them out of the book.
2. Tape them together so that they look like the ones below.
3. After you tape them, you will have two board games, back to back. Cool.
4. Take them to a copy shop or school supply and have them coated.
5. While there, buy some dice. (You can use a coin as a marker to move around the board.)

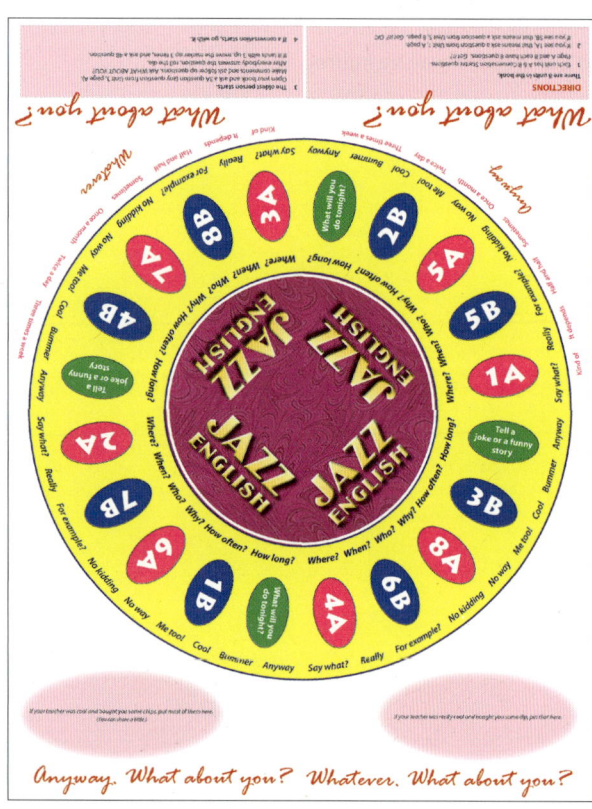

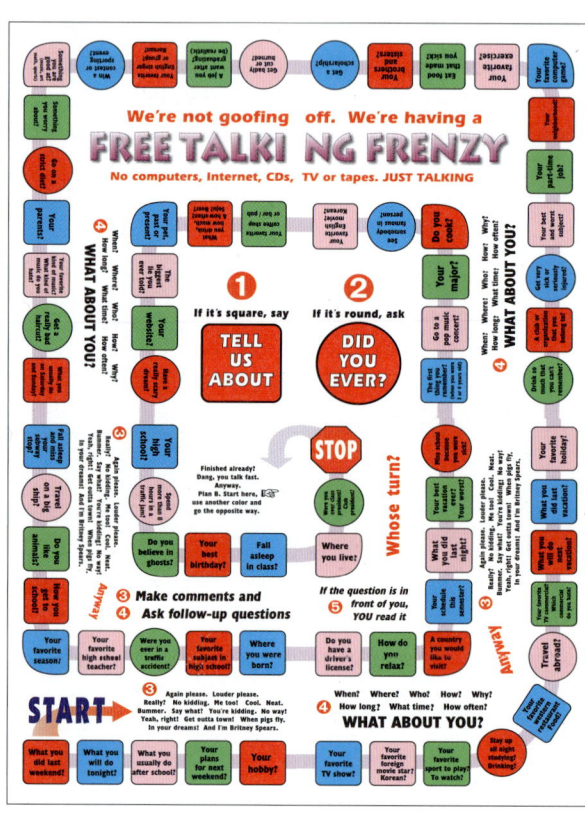

HOW TO
1. You can use the die and marker.
2. You can do this systematically:
   - Week 3: do the red questions.
   - Week 6: blue questions
   - Week 9: lavender questions
   - Week 12: green questions

1. The oldest person in the group asks the first question.
2. Everybody makes **comments** and asks **follow-up questions,** and asks **What about you?**
3. After EVERYBODY answers (about 5 - 10 minutes), roll the die and ask another question.
4. Each question is designed to start a conversation. If a conversation starts, **GO WITH IT!** Forget the game.
5. The first group to finish makes an F. If you finish quickly, you did not ask many follow-up questions.

130

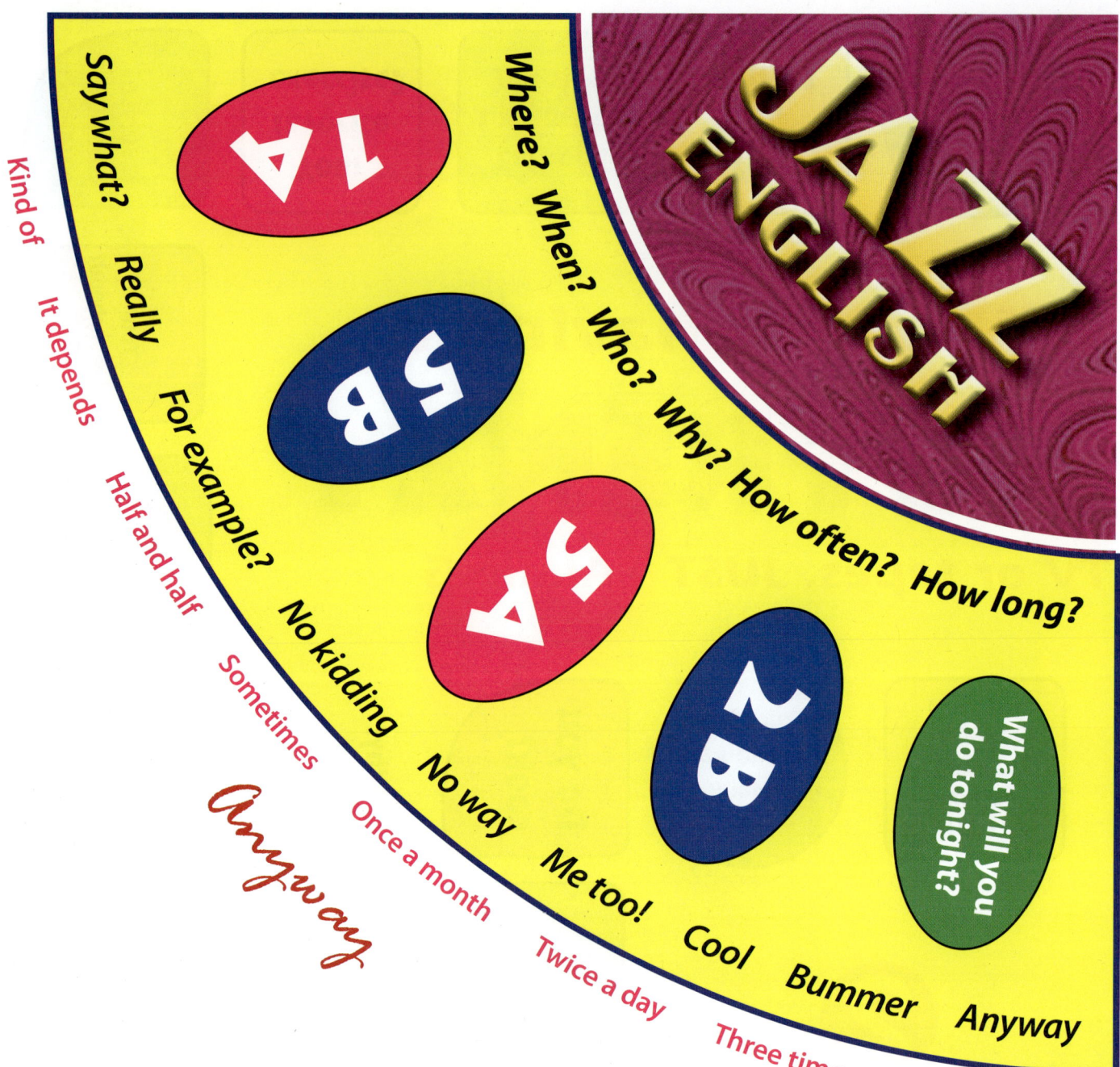

What about you?

DIRECTIONS

There are 8 units in the book.

1. Each unit has A & B Conversation Starter questions. Page A and B each have 8 questions. *Got it?*

2. If you see 1A, that means ask a question from Unit 1, A page. If you see 5B, that means ask a question from Unit 5, B page. *Got it? OK!*

3   **The oldest person starts.**
    Open your book and ask a 3A question (any question from Unit 3, page A).
    Make comments and ask follow-up questions. Ask WHAT ABOUT YOU?
    After everybody answers the question, roll the die.
    If it lands with 3 up, move the marker up 3 times, and ask a 4B question.

4   **If a conversation starts, go with it.**

WHAT ABOUT YOU?

④ How long? What time? How often?

When? Where? Who? How? Why?

Anyway

③ Again please. Louder please. Really? No kidding. Me too! Cool. Neat. Bummer. Say what? You're kidding! No way! Yeah, right! Get outta town! When pigs fly. In your dreams! And I'm Britney Spears.

⑤ If the question is in front of you, YOU read it

Whose turn?

STOP

- Your favorite TV show?
- Your favorite foreign movie star? Korean?
- Your favorite sport to play? To watch?
- Stay up all night studying? Drinking?
- Your favorite western restaurant? Food?
- Travel abroad?
- Your favorite TV commercial? Which commercial do you hate?
- What you will do next vacation?
- What you did last vacation?
- Your favorite holiday?
- Your best vacation ever? Your worst?
- Miss school because you were sick?
- What you did last night?
- Your schedule this semester?
- A country you would like to visit?
- How do you relax?
- Do you have a driver's license?
- Where you live?
- Were you ever class president? Club president?

START

What you did last weekend?

What you will do tonight?

What you usually do after school?

Your plans for next weekend?

Your hobby?

3
Again please. Louder please. Really? No kidding. Me too! Cool. Neat. Bummer. Say what? You're kidding. No way! Yeah, right! Get outta town! When pigs fly. In your dreams! And I'm Britney Spears.

Your favorite season?

Your favorite high school teacher?

Were you ever in a traffic accident?

Your favorite subject in high school?

Where you were born?

③ Make comments and ④ Ask follow-up questions

Anyway

How you get to school?

Do you like animals?

Travel on a big ship?

Fall asleep and miss your subway stop?

3
Again please. Louder please. Really? No kidding. Me too! Cool. Neat. Bummer. Say what? You're kidding! No way! Yeah, right! Get outta town! When pigs fly. In your dreams! And I'm Britney Spears.

Your high school?

Spend more than 8 hours in a traffic jam?

Do you believe in ghosts?

Your best birthday?

Fall asleep in class?

Finished already? Dang, you talk fast. Anyway. Plan B. Start here, use another color and go the opposite way.

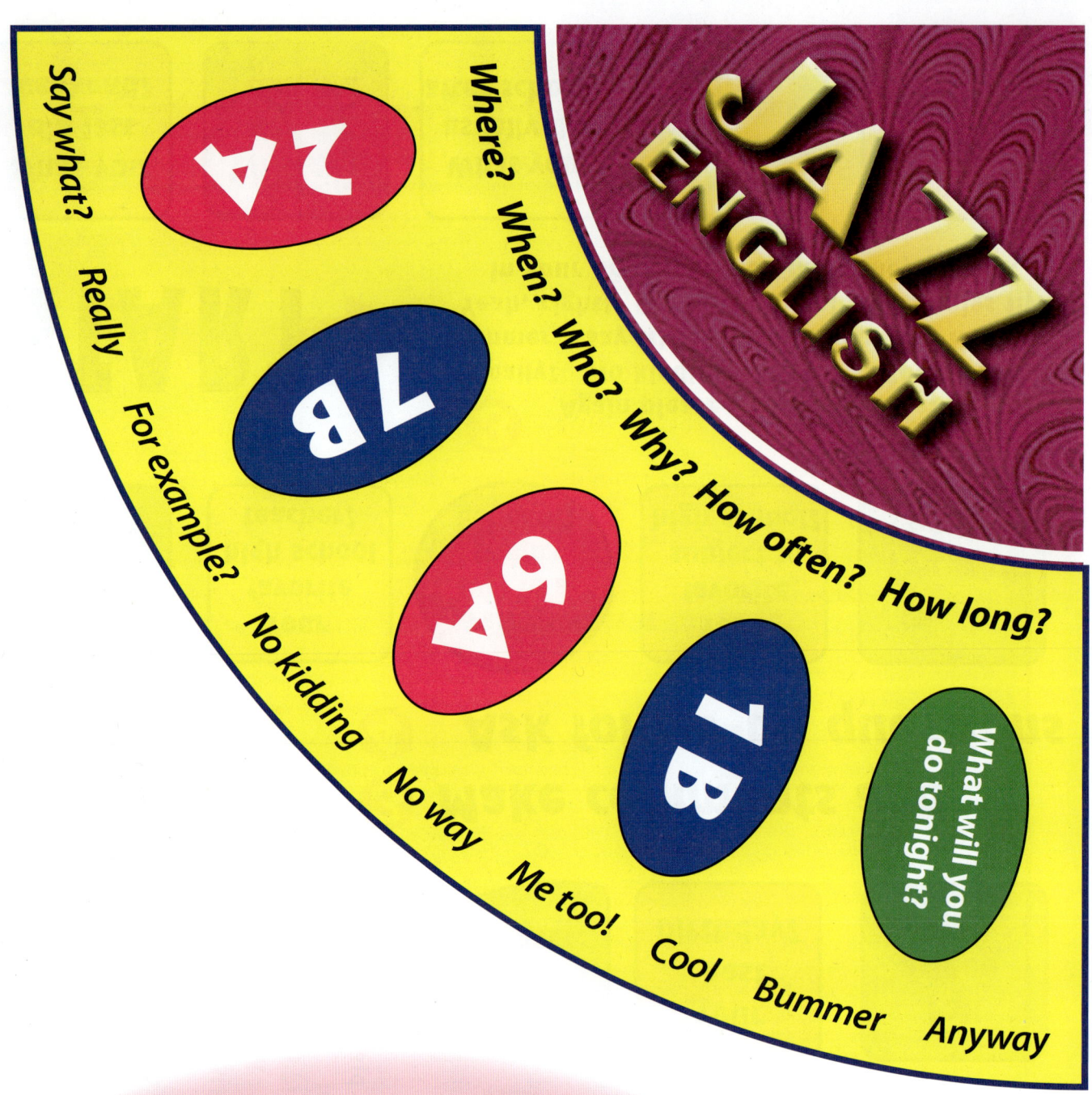

*If your teacher was cool and bought you some chips, put most of them here.
(You can share a little.)*

Anyway. What about you?

If your teacher was really cool and bought you some dip, put that here.

Whatever. What about you?

16 MAPS

1. WORLD　　　　　　　　　　140

2. USA　　　　　　　　　　　142

3. KOREA　　　　　　　　　　144

4. SEOUL　　　　　　　　　　146

Have you ever traveled abroad?

Where, when, who, how long?
Highlight where you have been.

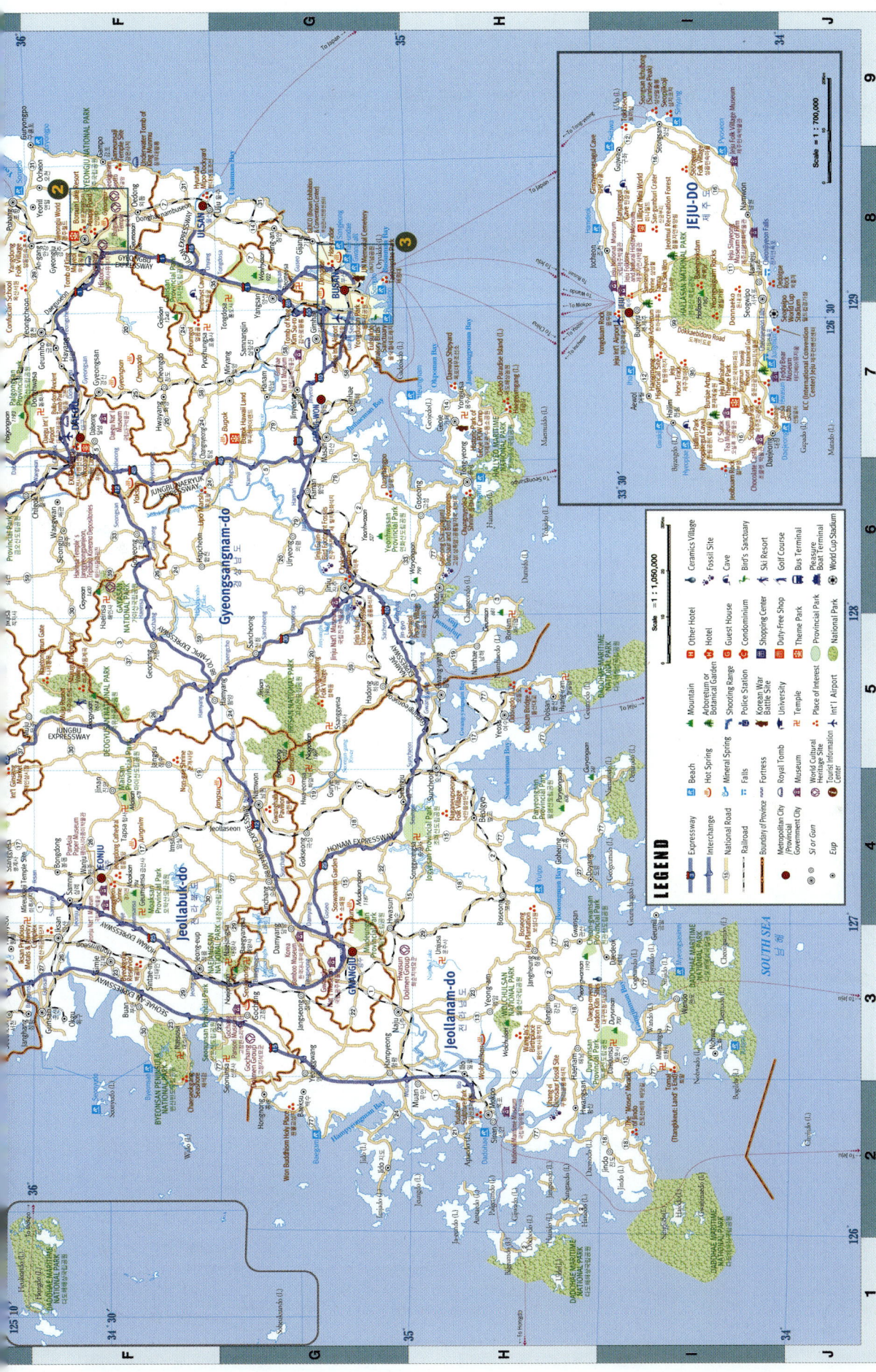

Notes

Notes